S0-DQV-957

03
795
2X5

The Family Symphony

VIRGINIA CLAWSON

BROADMAN PRESS
Nashville, Tennessee

© Copyright 1984 ● Broadman Press
All rights reserved
4256-61
ISBN: 0-8054-5661-9

Unless otherwise indicated, all Scripture quotations are from the King James Version of the Bible.

Dewey Decimal Classification: B
Subject Headings: CLAWSON, VIRGINIA //
CLAWSON, THOMAS WILLIAMS // CLAWSON, CYNTHIA

Library of Congress Catalog Card Number: 84-17524

Printed in the United States of America

Library of Congress Cataloging in Publication Data

Clawson, Virginia, 1928-
    The family symphony.

    1. Clawson family.   2. Clawson, Cynthia.   3. Christian
biography—United States.   4. Church music—United States.
5. Gospel music—United States.   I. Title.
BR1725.C514C43   1985   246'.7 [B]   84-17524
ISBN 0-8054-5661-9

Dedication

This book is lovingly and affectionately dedicated to Brother Tom: my childhood sweetheart, my husband, the father of our children, my pastor for twenty-four years, and my friend.

This book is a reality because he declared, "You can do it!" His support and editing of the stories after I had written them, with "Hey, don't forget, . . . " was exactly what I needed. While we have journeyed together for almost two score years, there have been many smiles and tears, but more than that, a new appreciation of the privilege that our Heavenly Father has walked with us and allowed us to serve Him. We praise Him for that.

It is also dedicated to our precious children, Cynthia, Patti, and Tommy, their spouses, and their children—for without them, there would be no *Family Symphony*.

Foreword

"Mary kept all of those things and pondered them in her heart"—and so did Mother.

To our knowledge Mary never wrote a book, and to our amazement, Mother has! The distillation of all our lives through the maternal memories of her heart has endeared her even more to us, her family.

She is one of God's innocents who, with a childlike faith and trust, has reared her children to love the Lord she so faithfully serves. She is the "virtuous woman" praised in Proverbs 31, and we are all the happier because of her.

She helped us to sing the music God planted in our hearts.

—CYNTHIA CLAWSON COURTNEY AND RAGAN COURTNEY

Contents

Prelude

This is not a "brag book"—nor is it a "how-to" book, but an attempt to show how music played a vital role in our family's life—and how necessary it is that we as parents enrich our children's lives with music and the opportunities to participate in one of God's most priceless gifts to mankind.

I do not want the reader to think that ours is the perfect and ideal family. It is as typical as any family in its problems, its experiences, its joys, and any future plans we might be able to carry out. Our children were of the "normal breed" with the usual needs and sibling rivalries that abound in the average household. God endowed each of them with gifts that needed developing, so we tried to provide opportunities for nurture. What is done with our gifts is extremely important.

Any gifts we may acquire are responsibilities on which we must build, to use them for God's glory and others' edification. I think C. H. Spurgeon was considering these responsibilities when he penned the words, "The one who takes the water to others, must go to the well more often."

We have endeavored to lead our children to be responsible for their gifts and also to remember that those gifts were God's, loaned to them, not achievements they themselves had piled up. We always asked them to lift their gifts up to the Heavenly Father for His approval and use.

I have not attempted to set down in chronological order each step we have taken thus far on our journey. Rather, using songs as a springboard for recalling precious memories, I have chosen to relate these stories topically.

Since I have written with songs in mind, it is because we are never without a song. We may hear, hum, or sing a certain song, and immediately the others will smile and start singing along because that song struck a chord in their hearts. At such times we all will recall a place, someone, or something.

Like a symphony, our life as a family has consisted of many movements; some to arrest our attention, as when God wanted to tell us something; other times, when we needed to listen and think on His will for our lives. Sometimes, we had to go through the valley only to find a beautiful mountaintop, where we truly could "Sing, Make a Joyful Sound."

Beatrice Bush Bixler wrote a song, "Life Is a Symphony," that explains what our life has become through the Great Arranger:

> Life is a symphony
> Since the Man of Galilee
> Changed my discord into song
> Made life sweet the whole day long.
>
> Life is a symphony
> Praise the Man of Galilee,
> No more a stranger
> He is the arranger of my symphony.[1]

This has been an exciting year for us as we have all looked back into our past while we called to remembrance the songs and happenings along our journey. Instead of looking into the fortune teller's crystal ball for a glimpse of the future, we have once again envisioned the pictures from our past. Like anyone else's life, the pictures are far too numerous to relate all, but we have merely touched on the highlights—those that relate to our song. Our story could not be told without the mention of a host of friends and acquaintances who have shared their lives and these experiences with us.

We are grateful to these and the vast number of friends not mentioned, because they have all played an important role in the Clawson family symphony—each playing their part to make this book a musical, autobiographical refrain.

We pray that you will accept this as a gift from our house to your house and consider it a little visit from us to you.

1
All God's Chill'uns Gotta Song

I gotta song, you gotta song,
All God's chill'uns gotta song,
When I get to Heaben,
I'm gonna sing a new song,
Goin' to sing all over God's Heaben.[2]

As much as we love this old spiritual, we do not have to wait until we get to "Heaben" to sing our song. The fortieth Psalm declares in stanza 3 that those whom the Lord has lifted up, have had a new song put into their "mouth, even praise unto our God." Simultaneously with conversion, the Holy Spirit instills within the heart a melody unto the Lord that is to be expressed with the mouth.

If I understand correctly, it is the privilege and obligation of every born-again child of God to praise and bless the Lord through music and song. We have often heard, "Sure, you can sing, you're the singing Clawsons." But each believer can sing his song in his own way. It doesn't have to be a strong, well-trained voice to be used by the Holy Spirit. He can take our meager offering and bless untold numbers—don't forget the loaves and fishes of John 6.

Early in his career (1959), Evangelist Larry Taylor, when asked if he could carry a tune, replied, "Sure, I can carry a tune, I just can't unload it!" That is not a legitimate reason for not participating in music. I think of a friend of ours, who is what is called a monotone. Yet, she sings every song in a worship service and I can't take my eyes from her face, as I see such joy and real communing with the Father as she lifts her "gift" to Him. Reverend Paul Eaton, a friend of thirty years or so, has contended that he *cannot* sing, and therefore he whistles. He whistles as he studies; he whistles as he works; he whistles as he worships. As I listen to that beautiful, lilting whistling, I find myself doubting the probability that he cannot sing.

Charles Taylor, well-known Scottish evangelist of a generation ago, was another outstanding whistler. At times, he would lead the congregational singing during a revival, with his melodious and unusual whistling. You might consider yourself as a squeaky soprano or a bumbling basso, and be shy about joining the chorus of voices in a worship service, so why not try whistling? That might be your medium to give vent to your song.

A song can be expressed not only with our voices, but with instruments as well. When King David brought the ark back to Jerusalem and placed it in the tent prepared for it, he "spake to the chief of the Levites to appoint their brethren to be the singers with instruments of music, psalteries and harps and cymbals, sounding, by lifting up the voice with joy (1 Chron. 15:16). He gave instructions to the priest and brethren to offer burnt offerings and praise to God. In 16:42 they were to use "trumpets and cymbals for those who should make a sound, and with musical instruments of God."

There are many great instrumentalists in the Christian fellowship. I think of our friend and long-time evangelist, Steve Taylor, who has for so long praised the Lord with his trumpet. Then, someone who has lately come up on the scene, Vernard Johnson. How he thrills and lifts us up, who sit and hear him pour out his very soul on the saxophone. You have to see him as he performs to feel his gift of worship as he plays and communes with his Father.

We are to let music speak *to* us as well as *through* us, helping us to "grow in grace, and in the knowledge of our Lord and Saviour Jesus Christ" (2 Pet. 3:18). Ephesians 5:19 says, "Speaking to yourselves in psalms and hymns and spiritual songs, singing and making melody in your heart to the Lord." Believing this, it is imperative that in every Christian home there be music that is Christ honoring, biblically sound, personally edifying, and enjoyable. It is equally important that no music, religious or secular, be allowed in the home that would dishonor Christ and be biblically unsound.

Before we understand how the contemporary Christian family does have a song to sing, we need to look through the Scriptures to see the impact of music on God's family.

The Christian faith is a singing faith. Music has been a vital part of worship since God first "laid the foundations of the earth" and "the morning stars sang together, and all the sons of God shouted for joy" (Job 38:4,7). Other instances as recorded in God's Word tell how Moses, Deborah, Barak, and David, among many others, sang their songs unto the Lord. Moses sang a song (Ex. 15:1-2). "Then sang Moses and the children of Israel this song unto the Lord, and spake, saying I will sing unto the Lord. . . . The Lord is my strength and song, and he is become my salvation: he is my God." Deborah and Barak lifted their voices in song (Judg. 5:1-2). "Then sang Deborah and Barak the son of Abinoam on that day, saying Praise ye the Lord for the avenging of Israel. . . . Hear, O ye kings; give ear, O ye princes; I, even I will sing unto the Lord; I will sing praise to the Lord God of Israel.' "

David, the sweet singer of Israel, poured out his heart in songs of praise, adoration, lament, and deliverance. Second Samuel 22 is one of the most beautiful songs portraying God as our Deliverer, our Rock, our Fortress, our Rewarder, our Lamp, our Strength, and our Power. David sang. "And David spoke unto the Lord the words of this song in the day that the Lord had delivered him out of the hand of all his enemies, and out of the hand of Saul" (v. 1). And in verse 50, "I will sing praises unto thy name." In Psalm 69:30 he cried, "I will praise the name of God with a song, and will magnify him with thanksgiving."

Mary's song forever rings in our hearts, as she sang out, "My soul doth magnify the Lord, And my spirit hath rejoiced in God my Saviour" (Luke 1:46-47). The proclamation of the angels as they sang, "Glory to God in the highest and on earth peace, good will toward men" (Luke 2:14), that night long ago, still echoes through the years and will go on as long as people celebrate the Savior's birth. Whenever the early Christians met, they sang for the joy of serving the Lord. Even in a Philippian jail, Paul and Silas sang a duet at midnight, singing praises to God, forgetting their predicament and danger. If many of us had been Paul's companion that night, he might have been singing a solo (Acts 16:25).

Today the possibilities for music are unlimited and in most homes, each child not only has the opportunity to hear, but usually has his or her own radio, TV, or record player to use for their own pleasure. Video music (MTV) is making an impact on the children of today, sometimes to their detriment. Here, the parent must guide what their children listen to and encourage each family member to share in an uplifting experience of music.

Each member may have their own favorite type of music, but this can be enjoyed by all and talked about in the family group. We must realize, however, that taste in music may be as varied as Joseph's coat of many colors. The younger members of the family may enjoy an upbeat, percussion-dominated record that leaves the older members cold and unresponsive—they may respond, though negatively. The country-western that thrills one family member may provoke, ridicule, and disgust another. The young operatic hopeful in the family would listen with disdain to "You Ain't Nothin' but a Hound Dog." The majestic hymn that so thrills the mature believer may leave the younger believer indifferent and unmoved. A home can be filled with music, and it is the obligation of each parent to provide what they can musically for their children.

Songs can be planted in the hearts of our children, long before they reach the age and time that God gives them the song of salvation, by our giving them a rich heritage of music. As a child I, like Larry Taylor, could not carry a tune, but I remember over and over my mother singing, "Carry Me Back to Old Virginny (Virginia)," and saying, "Now, you sing like I do. . . ." One line at a time, she would pattern the song for me and I would try. Most of the time I produced only "a joyful noise," but I kept on trying to mimic her tones.

Later, when I was eight, my father bought an old, second-hand upright piano for me and sent me to a piano teacher. As I played up the keyboard, 1-2-3, and down the keyboard, 1-2-3, I sang each note, and for the first time really heard the tone that Mother had worked so patiently for me to hear.

And we also had the radio. Mother would keep it tuned to musical programs during the day and we would sing along together. Remember the songs of the 1930's—"The Music Goes Round and Round . . . and it comes out here," "Carolina Moon," "My Blue Heaven," "Now's the Time to Fall in Love," and many others?

I could not have known when I got my first piano that it would become one of the loves of my life and would play a vital part in my life. As long as I can remember, I had wanted to play the piano, and I finally convinced my father that I would practice if only he would find me a piano. He made arrangements for one, but it required a month or so to get it. In the meantime, Mother had enlisted a piano teacher, and I began my lessons without a piano on which to practice. My teacher's home was en route to school, and I would go early each morning to practice on her piano and return after school for more study when she was not having lessons. I remember also using the kitchen table to practice holding my hands correctly and running the scales up and down, without a sound. I didn't need a keyboard—I had the sound in my heart.

By the time I was eleven, I was playing in Sunday School. The summer I was thirteen I was elected church pianist by a church of 2,000 members, while my piano teacher, who was the pianist, took a leave of absence. I realized then that playing the piano was to be my chief service for the Lord the rest of my life.

It is never too early to introduce music into the life of a child. Today there are so many remarkable musical toys for even the bed babies. Our children learned to sleep with the radio on or my piano playing. When the children were very young, we bought a small inexpensive record player, one they could operate without our help, and provided many children's records and religious records that told stories, as well as "sing-a-longs." They spent many happy hours sitting on the floor with their records stacked according to their favorites. We can still hear "Happy Trails to You," "Sam-u-el," "Me and My Teddy Bear," "Open Up Your Heart," and "Jesus Wants Me for a Sunbeam."

We sang with our children all the time—as we worked, as we played, as we traveled in the car. Tom was their voice teacher and I their piano teacher. He sings or whistles all day long. Like Cynthia, our eldest child, he is never without a song. Songs flow from him like a never-ending well—all kinds of songs. One of our deacons, Volley Broom, used to say, "Brother Tom, I always know when you are coming. I hear your whistling or singing." He seems to have a song for every occasion, and if he doesn't, he'll make up one, to the children's delight. As he read to them when they were young, they especially liked the poems because, more than likely he would burst forth in song, creating his own melody.

As soon as the children could sit at the piano, I began to guide their fingers along the keyboard in tunes they would enjoy. About the age of four, each child began to study music seriously and later, when I felt it was time, we arranged for them to study under another teacher. Sometimes it is hard for one to teach piano to one's own children. We often put them off until our work is done. Sometimes there is little continuity in the study, because we do not keep a close schedule. And we often do not pay as close attention as we should.

This came home to us when Cynthia was five years old. We were in college then, and we made arrangements for her to study under one of the students who was majoring in music, Lois Venable. Lois is now Mrs. Maurice Marrow. She and Maurice are Southern Baptist foreign missionaries in Tanzania. After several lessons, Lois came to me and said, "Do you know that Cynthia doesn't know her line and spaces? She is playing what I play. She is memorizing the tune."

Because she had been playing all the beginner songs in the first-grade book, I had been confident that she was "reading" the music as well as playing. Needless to say, Cynthia received a "crash" course in how to read music.

"All God's Chill'uns Gotta Song," but in some He implants a special ability. When our children came into the world, we could not possibly have known their special gifts, but as each came along, the gift became manifest at different times and in different ways. Cynthia was only a few months old when we heard a variant type of "cooing" coming from her crib; to our amazement she was making melodies. She hummed a tune long before she spoke any words. By the time she was three years old, she sang her first solo in church—as clear-voiced and on perfect pitch as any well-trained singer. She sang from the time she arose in the morning, all day long, and at night would sing herself to sleep, usually hitting a high note and drifting off to slumberland at that point.

Many years later, as we were going over the plans for her marriage to Ragan Courtney, I laughingly remembered, "Ragan, I hope you like music. Cynthia usually sings herself to sleep."

When they returned from their honeymoon, Ragan reported, "You were right! I didn't believe you when you told me that a grown young lady would sing herself to sleep, but she did—and—me, too."

Four years after Cynthia was born came Patti, and she had her big sister as a pattern. She loved to sing as well. She would try so hard to follow along, but her words fell all over themselves.

At first, when Patti learned to talk, we were afraid that something was terribly wrong, because she had such a time pronouncing her words. We even carried her to a speech correction teacher to see if something really needed developing. Later, when we placed her in kindergarten, I asked the teacher to evaluate her and let us know what we could do. I found that I was the typical mother hen and objected to what she told us: "Oh, that's just baby talk, and we can get her out of that!" Anyway, this was a part of Patti's charm as a baby.

When she was about three, one of her favorite songs was, "I too lung to mard in the invery" (translation: "I'm Too Young to March in the Infantry"). If she couldn't hit all the high notes, she might simply start whistling (her brand), like the time she was singing in the "Booster Band" at a revival in King City, California. The children were singing:

> Are we downhearted? No! No!
> Are we downhearted? No! No!
> Troubles may come, troubles may go
> We trust in Jesus come weal or woe,
> Are we downhearted [Whistle] No! No! No![3]

When they came to the whistle part, it was too high, so Patti in perfect pitch cut loose with her substitute whistle—"EE EEE No! No! No!" She brought the house down. So, whether the tones or words are correct, it's still a "song."

Our son, Tommy, made his appearance four years after Patti. He enjoyed listening to his sisters sing. As we all gathered around the piano to sing, he would pat his feet, keeping time to the rhythm. He was about eleven months old when we discovered his ability to do this. His daddy was playing the guitar, and I turned around to see the baby had pulled himself up to the door facing and was holding on with one hand. It looked like an electric charge was running up one leg and down the other as he felt the rhythm of the music.

When he was three, he attempted his first solo in church. I say "attempted" because that is precisely what it amounted to. He said one day,

"Daddy, the girls sing in church all the time. Why can't I?" Well, sounded like a good idea to us, so we began to prep him with "Jesus Loves Me."

At that time, Brother Tom was pastoring a small country church outside Yoakum, Texas—our first time in the country. Since the services were rather informal and there were several families with small children, the children were given opportunities to express their "songs," usually on Sunday or Wednesday nights. So, on the appointed Wednesday night, Brother Tom announced to the congregation that Tommy had a song. Tommy got up with all the confidence in the world and stood by his daddy. When he turned around, I suppose he thought he was looking at an audience of 10,000, instead of the small congregation in that small country church. He opened his mouth, but nothing came out. He looked toward me at the piano, as I started playing; then, up at his daddy. He grabbed his daddy by the leg and literally melted down to the floor. Brother Tom, stooping to retrieve his soloist, remarked, "Well, he had a song, but I believe he will try again some other time."

God gives a song, but can we lose it? Not really, but many things can block that song—fear, anxiety, disappointment, among other things. Cynthia lost her song only one time I remember. She was four years old, when we moved to Corpus Christi, Texas, to enroll in the University of Corpus Christi, the only Baptist school in South Texas at that time. (It now is a part of the state system of Texas A & I.)

The move was a more traumatic experience for Cynthia than we had realized. She had to leave the security of the only home she had ever known, her beloved grandparents and other family members, and her little friends. We had tried to include her in all of our plans concerning the move, even letting her help pick out the apartment we would live in on the college campus. We talked about the new friends she would make and the new house we would have, but this was not enough for her.

After we moved, there were busy days becoming settled, enrolling immediately in the spring semester, putting Cynthia in kindergarten, and getting Patti, age six months, in the nursery.

Some time passed before we noticed that Cynthia was not singing. She seemed happy enough, but there was no song. I remember the day this dawned on me, and I told Tommy that something had to be done. She needed her song back, and we certainly needed to hear her sing again!

He asked, "What can we do?" We felt so strongly about her happiness that we contemplated going back to Houston and enrolling in a school there, if she was so miserable. We tried to interest her in singing—but to no avail. And then it happened. The day came when, as she ran through the kitchen and out the back door, I heard her singing one of her favorite songs at the top of her lungs. Some way, she had worked it all out by herself and her song has not stopped since!

Recently, Patti commented, "You know, Mother, you used to tell us that if we didn't use our 'song,' that the Lord would take it from us. I don't quite agree with that. The Lord won't take it away entirely, but atrophy through lack of exercise can cause you to lose control of your voice, and you can lose the effectiveness." I began to think about it, for that had always been a fear of mine, especially in my teen years—that something would happen to my hands and I would not be able to play the piano. Patti was saying that if we do not use the ability God gives us, whether it is to sing, to teach, or simply to share the gospel with a friend, these gifts will become dull, corroded, rusty like a new nail left out in the rain. I have seen this happen. Although God gives the gift, He expects us to polish it, to increase it, and make it beautiful. We can't lose our song, but we might (like Archie Bunker says) "Stifle it!"

When Tommy surrendered to preach we went to college, and his burning desire was to proclaim God's message of salvation from a pulpit —any pulpit would do. But because of his beautiful voice, the calls came to sing rather than to preach. He does enjoy singing because, as he so often says, "If I couldn't sing, I believe I would simply 'pop.' " But he still wanted to preach more than all else.

One night, after we had been there a couple of months, Cynthia asked, "Daddy, aren't you supposed to be a preacher?"

"Yes, honey, why do you ask?"

"Well," said Cynthia, with a puzzled look on her face, "if you are, then why don't you preach?"

He laughed and replied, "That's what I've been asking myself."

That night, after we put the girls to bed, we talked about her question. Tommy said, "You know, I've become known as a singer, and that is not why we came to college. I think the next time someone asks me to sing, I'll tell them I'll come if I can preach, but not to sing."

I quickly replied, "Oh, you can't do that. God will take away your singing voice. It's true, you've been called to preach, but you have another gift—your voice—and you must find a way to use both."

He told me later that John McLaughlin, our friend who was then educational director of the Downtown Baptist Church where we were members, had also warned him about not giving up singing. John had commented playfully, but in dead earnest, "Tom, you better use it or lose it."

Finally, Tom did receive some calls to preach, but his singing voice began to give him trouble. It had a raspy sound, a "dull and rusty" sound; and he realized that the Lord was trying to give him a message— "Tom, I want you to sing for me, also."

He began to pray sincerely, "Lord, give me back my song, and I'll do anything You want me to do." And, the Lord heard and answered, giving him back the ability to sing with a clear, strong voice. He found avenues for using both his speaking and singing gifts. Sometimes when he is preaching he may break into song to illustrate a point. This surely does wake up the sleepyheads in the congregation.

His ability to sing has come in handy. Often the church might be small and there would be no song leader, so he would "doublehead" and lead the music as well as preach. I remember our first tiny mission down in the wharf area of Corpus Christi. The congregation met in the downstairs apartment of a two-story house. After that first Sunday we were there, I told Tommy that he was certainly the whole show. He taught the adult Sunday School class, led the singing, took up the offering, sang a solo, preached the sermon, and gave the invitation!

"I gotta song, you gotta song." Yes, we do. As travelers on the Christian pilgrimage, so many people fail to look for God's handiwork along the path and miss the blessings of God's gifts in nature. Just so, people not attuned to God's song fail to hear the message given to the songwriters, and thus miss receiving the gift of music. God does speak to us through music and words as He has down through the centuries. Many times a songwriter will express a deep spiritual feeling that we share and are unable to put into words, so we exclaim, "I wish I could put it into words like that."

We must find a way to express our song, to let it grow in our hearts, and to share it with others. Life would indeed be a dreary, weary place "Without a Song."

2
God Gave the Song

Come walk with me thru fields and forests
We'll climb the hills and still hear that song.
For even hills resound with music
They just can't help it,
God gave the song.[4]

I am a romantic! I believe that marriages are made in heaven. In a sense this is true, for God has a plan for our lives from birth to death; therefore, the one He chooses for our life's partner is surely in His blueprint for our lives. The Lord created man and then said, "It is not good for the man to be alone; I will make him a helper suitable for him" (Gen. 2:18, NASB). So, it is not just a coincidental crossing of two paths when we meet the person God has already planned for us. When we do this in our youth, the union becomes something on which we can build a lifetime.

"The Clawson Clan," as we often jokingly call our family, began when a young man crawled through the window of a Sunday School room to talk with two young girls. He should have been in the worship service and not prowling around. Velna Nelson and I had been elected to lead the Sunbeams during the morning church services, with the stipulation that we keep the door locked so none of the children could "escape."

Tommy had left the service, presumably for a drink of water. Hearing the singing coming from the educational building, and wanting to see Velna anyway, he came to the door, tried the handle, and was surprised to find it locked. We told him that we could not open the door, so he proceeded to climb through the window. I had him confused with another boy in the church, and I went home telling Mother that I had met that crazy boy, Tom Goolsby. How was I to know that Tom was the one God had picked for me? Tommy was fifteen and I was thirteen.

In the months that followed, we became aware of each other as our paths began to intermingle. We were both active in the youth activities in our church. It wasn't long before we became a "pair." A little young, you say? Yes, but all our "dating" was done at church and get-togethers or at one of our homes, well supervised. We didn't have any money to date, anyway.

Even in those early days, music played a paramount part in our lives. Gene, one of our friends a couple of years older than we, led the music in the intermediate department of Sunday School. Tommy's aunt was the director of the department, and she let Gene have "free rein" with the music for the opening exercises. The first thing he did was to organize a choir (this was in the days before youth choirs) and he selected a corner of the room for his singers. He not only worked with us on Sunday mornings but had choir practice during the week. Since I had been elected the pianist for the department and Tommy was singing in the choir, we began to see each other with different eyes. He was a big tease and joke teller and kept the group always in an uproar, but we did manage to study music.

We might have been "playing" at choir, but we learned much about the rudiments of music and the fundamentals of working together in a group. It was not long until we were asked to sing at different churches and for special occasions. Each month we sang at the Star of Hope Mission, a mission for street people in downtown Houston, and at the Harris County Home for the Aged—both real mission fields.

I think we received the greater blessing as we tried not only to share our music, but our Christian friendship as well. I remember how those dear old people in the home for the aged would sit with smiles on their weather-worn, ancient faces, often with eyes closed, rocking back and forth as they were carried many years back into their pasts, while they listened to us sing: "The Old Rugged Cross," "Amazing Grace," and "Rock of Ages."

We can still recall some of the songs and choruses we learned in that first choir experience. Usually every emphasis in church, whether in Sunday School or Baptist Training Union (as it was called then) had a special song to reinforce the theme. Generally, this was a parody on some well-known tune; for instance, "I Want to be a Tither for the Lord" and "Winning Intermediates" by B. B. McKinney to the music for "Bringing in the Sheaves." As these simple songs were woven into the texture of our lives, they became an impetus to help us form a value system. Many of these songs and choruses have remained a part of our church music heritage, and we in turn have taught them to our children as soon as they could talk. Now they are passing them on to their children. Many of the little choruses are classics, and what a thrill it is to hear our grandchildren singing the same songs I taught those early Sunbeams to sing.

Tommy and I were both from Christian homes, active in the church and community. Our dads were hard-working men, who did not bring home much money from their long hours of labor. These were the years prior to the Second World War, and all our friends were of similar circumstances. Our mothers were busy in "church work"; both were teachers in the Sunday School and leaders in the organizations of the church. Both also sang in the choir. This often proved to be rather hard on Tommy and me, as they watched us from the choir loft. If they thought we were talking or making excessive movements, one or the other would clear her throat and give us a reprimanding look. In order to get around that, Tommy and I joined the adult choir, but since we couldn't sit together we weren't always as faithful as the choir director wanted us to be. He would often stand at the beginning of the service, look over the congregation, and observe, "I see several of our choir members sitting out there. We need you up here." At this, Tommy and I would try to duck under the seat in front of us.

Tommy's mother was gifted with an unusually gorgeous voice and sang most of the soprano solo parts in the choir specials, and his daddy sang in the bass section. Tommy came from a large family of aunts, uncles, and cousins, and the choir would often be filled with those good singers.

One of the true milestones in my early teen years (age thirteen) was being asked to sing in the Christmas cantata with the adult choir.

Since money was scarce in our families, we had to invent ways we could be together without spending any money. Tommy has never ceased being amazed at how during those years of almost dire circumstances, my mother had the gift of always making provisions for unexpected guests at the dining room table. This, coupled with her ability to provide refreshments for an impromptu youth fellowship after service on Sunday nights, was almost miraculous. Taking whatever she had on hand, she would often surprise us with the most delectable snacks. Tom never has forgotten the night Mother urged, "Oh, don't rush off. I'm making fried pies for everyone." Call it "Southern hospitality" or what, she was given a gift from God, and she exercised it whenever the opportunity arose.

One of our favorite pastimes was gathering at my house on Sunday afternoon because I had a piano. The house, full of young people, would pulsate with the sound of music as we gathered around that same old upright Daddy had bought me when I was eight years old. Someone would sit on the sofa, going through the stack of sheet music, picking out their favorites and yelling, "Do this one next." Tommy reserved the place on the piano bench beside me for himself, and two of his favorites were "oldies"—"Little Girl Dressed in Blue" and "I Found a Million Dollar Baby . . . in a 5 and 10 cent store. . . ." Some may remember: "You're the Only Star in My Blue Heaven," "San Antonio Rose," "By the Light of the Silvery Moon," and "Shine On, Harvest Moon."

These old songs have become as much a part of our children's lives as they were of ours. Someone once asked Cynthia, when she sang one of the "oldies but goodies" songs, where in the world had she heard *that* one? and she replied, "My Daddy taught it to me."

The so-called "popular" song was born in America, straight from the American heart, and expressed the joys, sorrows, dreams, and hopes of the American people. There seems to be one for every occasion, and as our memories run through the halls of music, recalling far too many to list, some simply must be mentioned, like: "I'm Just a Prisoner of Love," "The Gypsy," "Always," and "The Band Played On."

These were the songs Tommy would sing to me on our dates, before and after World War II, serenading me like the lovers of olden times. Sometimes he would reach way back to songs like "Girl of My Dreams, I Love You, Honest, I Do" and "Carolina Moon." He was never without a song.

There is an old song, "Wedding Bells Are Breaking Up That Old Gang of Mine," but this wasn't true of "our gang" which sang around the piano on Sunday afternoons. It was the war—World War II. As we said good-bye to the boys, our songs became—"I'll Be Back in a Year, Little Darling," "I Wish That I Could Hide Inside This Letter," "As Time Goes By," "Harbor Lights," and we learned all the songs of the different branches of the service—"The Marine Corps Hymn," "Anchors Away," "The Army Air Corps," "You're in the Army Now," "The Caissons Go Rolling Along," and others. When the war was over, the boys that went away came back men, and our lives were never the same.

Tommy was one of the last in our gang to return, since his group had been sent to China to accept the surrender of the Japanese there, and by the time he reached home, it had been almost four years since we had seen each other! But the love was still there and we immediately began talking of marriage. I accepted his ring and plans for a fall wedding were made.

During the war I had continued my studies in music with the main emphasis on classical and church music, while his choice of listening and participating had been somewhat limited, due to three years in the South Pacific. What he did enjoy listening to the most was what is now known as country-western. He recalls the singing sessions that the men in his Marine company would hold when they would gather around at night accompanied by guitar and harmonica. The majority of these men were from the South and Southwest, and their songs would naturally take on the flavor of those regions. They were able to keep up with the latest popular songs being sung back home, and he remembers walking down a moonlit-bathed South Pacific beach singing: "I'm Gonna Buy a Paper Doll That I Can Call My Own . . . a doll that other fellows cannot steal. . . ."

After coming home and listening to my type of music, he would merely sit politely and endure my playing a concerto or a Bach impromptu, not understanding it at all.

One day I suggested that we attend the concert in the park. During the summers in Houston, the symphony orchestra gave concerts in an outdoor theater in Herman Park (I think they still do), and I had attended every one I could.

He queried, "You mean, some of that highbrow music—all that squeaky-violin stuff? No, thank you."

I tried to explain how nice it was and finally one word caught his attention—*BLANKET;* I commented that we usually carried a blanket and sat on the grass. Later, he admitted that he thought, *Boy, she's changed a lot—a BLANKET party—Wow!"*

We attended the following night, and as he listened to the symphonic music floating on the clear air, he said, "You know, this isn't bad at all." But I didn't completely win him over that night.

Later, we attended a concert given by Sigmund Romberg and Tom came away singing, "One Alone," "Romance," and the "Desert Song." His world was opening to new fields of music.

I must admit I was rather prejudiced against his favorite music— country-western—and it wasn't until after we married (and I had to listen to "Way Back in the Hills," "Way Down Yonder in the Indian Nation," or "Bonaparte's Retreat" every morning before we went to work) that I learned a new appreciation for the grass roots of American music.

On November 16, 1946, six years after the time when Tommy crawled through that window in Park Memorial Baptist Church, we stood at the altar while "Always . . . I'll be loving you, always" was being sung. When our pastor asked of us our desires, we pledged our lives forever to be one, and the song of our life together began. We not only pledged to each other, but we vowed that God would be the center of our lives. For even then, not knowing all the doors on God's blueprint that would open to us, we wanted His song to be sung in our lives.

> Come walk with me through fields and forests
> We'll climb the hills and still hear that song,
> For even hills resound with music
> They just can't help it,
> God gave the song.

We had plenty of growing to do, much yielding to God's will, and a lot of learning about His Word before He would open many doors for us—and finally, the *one* door that would change our entire lives.

Nothing stood still around the Clawson household, even from the beginning. We went from one crisis to the next, certainly not all bad, but often life-changing steps for us. God blessed us with a beautiful red-haired baby girl, Cynthia Dee, and we could not have possibly known what a blessing she would become to millions who listen to her song—God's song. She came with a song. But we had to give her opportunities to expand and explore that song and provide her with a foundation of all kinds of music.

After four years of marriage, Tommy was called back into the Marine Corps when the Korean War broke out, and our lives changed drastically. He reported to Camp Pendleton, California, on October 20, 1950, and Cynthia and I remained at home until he was settled. We joined him in January, taking up residence in Fallbrook, California.

On the first Sunday we attended the First Baptist Church, a most unusual church. It was affiliated with the American Baptist Convention because of a debt owed to them. Their missionary money was channeled through the Conservative Baptist Convention. Its pastor had been a nondenominational missionary behind the Iron Curtain, and the people were also interested in the Southern Baptist program. I wrote home that it was a good-old-gospel-loving Baptist church.

When we attended the first service, we walked in a few minutes late and found they were having a request night for the singing. There weren't many there—perhaps thirty or so—and as we sang, of course, Tommy's strong voice boomed out above the whole congregation. He requested a certain number and the lady who was leading the music asked, "Sir, I don't believe we know that one. Would you please come and pattern it for us?"

This completely threw Tommy, because he had never sung a solo before, other than serenading me. I whispered to him, "Go on. You can do it."

So, being the brave Marine he was, he walked down the aisle to the front of the church. As he was singing, Cynthia began calling for her daddy, and before I could grab her, she was out and running down the aisle, as fast as her plump, two-year-old legs would carry her. I ran after her and caught her right before she reached Tommy. When he returned and sat down beside me, I leaned over and asked, "Wasn't Cynthia just terrible?"

He whispered back, "What did she do?"

"Why, she ran down the aisle, screaming for you, and I caught her just before she got to you."

"Well, I didn't see her," he answered. He had been so nervous that everything else had been blocked out. We still laugh about his first solo, but God opened a door that night. He had been wanting Tommy to use his talent, and now was the time.

God was working out His "score" for our lives, even through these experiences and this uprooting of our lives. After a short six-month stint in the Marines we stood one April day with a medical discharge in our hands. They had discovered that Tommy had a duodenal ulcer in the last stages, and instead of treating him there in the Navy hospital, they were sending him home to his family doctor.

We had made many good friends in our short stay at Fallbrook. It wasn't hard to see what a mission field California was and we wanted to stay but needed to go home worse.

We had bought a 1932 Ford in San Diego for sightseeing and never dreamed of driving it home. But when the time came, we decided to drive it back to Texas. We would keep back enough money as we went along for a bus ticket in case it broke down. You ask what is so strange about driving a car to Texas. Well, the first thing, the car was nineteen years old; we hadn't had it long enough to test it; and Tommy knew very little about a car. He hadn't owned a car when he was younger, when most boys learn by experience to fix a car. As for tools, we had a pair of pliers, a hammer, and one odd-size wrench.

But we were young and foolish, or perhaps we had explicit faith in God. We were to learn later there is an extremely fine line dividing faith from foolishness. So, early one morning, we drove out of town, all three singing, "So Long, It's Been Good to Know You . . . but we gotta be drifting along." We promised ourselves to return someday.

Miraculously, the car did carry us home, 2,000 miles and six days later, with no trouble but a fan belt that unraveled and broke as we drove into a filling station in Yuma, Arizona, and one tire that went flat as we were gassing up in Hobbs, New Mexico.

I laugh when I hear the phrase, "Meanwhile, back on the ranch," but that is a good Texas expression, and it was true for us. Back home, we once again entered into the mainstream of life as it had been when we left six months before. We couldn't help wondering why our lives were disturbed for only six months and why we had to go to California, but God was leading us toward another one of His doors.

Tommy added to his service for the Lord with his voice; he now had enough confidence to sing specials in the worship services, or wherever he was asked. Of course, I had to play the piano, and he would practice for a number of hours before he was to sing. He couldn't read music then and does so only moderately now, but he had a lovely voice. People have always been blessed.

Almost a year had gone by before he was given his first opportunity to lead the music in a revival. Our pastor had recommended him to the pastor of a neighboring church. Brother Williams called one morning and asked if Tommy would lead the music in their coming meeting, and I answered, "He's never done that before, but I know he can. I will have to play for him, though." Brother Williams assured that would be no problem, and he would count on us.

When Tommy came in from work that afternoon, I exulted, "Guess what? You're going to lead the singing in a revival. Brother Williams from Oldham Memorial Baptist Church called this morning to ask if you would help them out in their revival. And I told him you would."

He looked at me with amazement and came back with, "You're kidding! I can't do that. How did this Brother Williams get my name? We don't know him." I told him that our pastor had recommended him, so he must think Tom could do it, and I knew he could.

We were about to go through another of God's doors—the most important one.

The evangelist was Dr. Harry A. Marko, a converted Jew (the term used then). He was an itinerant missionary to the Jewish people of Texas and was affiliated with the American Board of Missions to the Jews. We had not heard of him before. As we listened each night, we realized that we had never heard such prophetic preaching, and we knew that the Holy Spirit was at work in our hearts in an unusual manner. Tommy was very nervous at the beginning of the week, but as the nights passed he relaxed and seemed so natural that the people responded to his directing and his singing. Each day we could hardly wait for the next service.

On Friday night, we arrived there a little early, and when Dr. Marko came in, he asked Tommy to go with him into the pastor's study. They talked for a long time and when Tommy came out, he was as white as a sheet. I could not imagine what had transpired and asked, "What's the matter?" Tommy replied, trembling, "That man says that God is calling me to preach!"

First, Dr. Marko had asked Tom how much schooling he had. Tom told him—just high school—that after graduation in 1942, he had gone immediately into the Marine Corps, where he had spent almost four years, had returned, and married. Then, Dr. Marko asked him if he had ever felt a call to do special service for the Lord.

Tommy told him, "You know, that's funny! I guess I have. One time I thought I would like to be an educational director because I love the educational part of Sunday School. I even 'put out the fleece' once, but didn't feel any particular leading of the Lord. No doors seem to have opened."

"Well," said Dr. Marko, "sit down, I have some news for you. God is calling you to preach. Last night, I was praying and a vision came to me concerning you. I don't want you to rush into anything without first talking to the Lord, but promise me that you will seek His will in this matter."

You know, in all the years that followed, and with our close relationship with Dr. Marko, we never did ask him what he had meant by a "vision" and exactly what he saw.

We were awed by the prospect of what all this would entail, and that night as we drove home, we began to talk about the possibility that Dr. Marko might be right. For six years, we had known God was dealing in our lives and that there must be more He wanted us to do, but this was the farthest thought from our minds. Tommy had commented several times, "You know, I would like to be a preacher, but God could not use me to stand in His pulpit."

There are many ways we can sing our song for the Lord, and each fulfills a mission for Him. The most important facet is to know *where* He wants us to sing.

In the months that followed, we prayed much, together and separately, and asked our pastor and friends to pray with us. We grew in our study of the Word as we tried to find the answer. The revival had been in February of 1952, and it wasn't until the last of October that we finally came to take this new step in our service for the Lord. We were certainly not rebelling against a call during those weeks and months, but we simply had to be sure, for this would mean a radical change in every aspect of our lives.

We began to have a peace that we had never known before. All things began to fall into their rightful places. God's will, like a new book with its many unread pages, began opening before our eyes. We received assurances almost daily, from all sides, that this was His will for us.

Three special men from our childhood, upon hearing that Tommy had surrendered to preach, confessed, "I've known for a long time that God wanted you to preach." We laughingly said, "Well, why didn't you tell us about it?" One was our former pastor, Brother Bill Shuttlesworth who had married us; another, Russell Payne, a great prayer warrior from our home church; and my grandfather, W. C. Lowery, a retired Baptist minister.

During these months of searching and growing in the Lord He gave us another gift—a lovely blond-haired, blue-eyed, baby girl—Patti Jean. It was such a joy to watch Cynthia with her new baby sister. She would stand over her bassinet, holding Patti's tiny hand, and sing to her. Then, Cynthia would ask, "When can she sing with me?" And they have done that for over thirty years.

From the night Dr. Marko had talked with Tommy, we realized that such a step would mean our preparing spiritually, emotionally, and educationally for the ministry. Spiritually and emotionally was no problem for us, for we were on "cloud nine." Our prayer was, in the words of Johnson Oatman:

> Lord, lift me up and let me stand,
> By faith, on heaven's table land,
> A higher plane than I have found;
> Lord, plant my feet on higher ground.

That night as we left the church Tommy had said, "You know what this means—I'll have to go to college and I'm twenty-eight years old. Do you think we can?"

This was a tremendous admission for him, because I had begged him to enter school when he was first out of the service. He could have used his G. I. bill, but he had declared that only doctors and lawyers need to go to school, and he certainly wasn't going to be one of those.

"I don't know how we'll do it, but we'll go," Tom affirmed.

We had no savings, had just come through a two-and-a-half months' strike at Shell Chemical, where Tommy worked, and had watched all our Savings Bonds dwindle away as we used them to survive those weeks without a paycheck.

We began claiming Romans 8:28, even in the beginning, with the assurance that God would provide our every need, and if He wanted us to enter college, He would see that we had the wherewith. We would, of course, sell our home and garner a small equity from that, and the only other tangible assets we had were our furniture and our car—a 1932 Ford.

Sometimes we receive answers to our questions during our lifetime, but sometimes we will have to wait until heaven, but the Lord had an answer to our question, "Why six months out of our life for the Korean War and California?" all wrapped up in His call to the ministry.

A week or so after Tommy made his decision and had told the church, I found his envelope of military papers in a drawer as I was cleaning. I decided to see what was there. My eyes fell on a letter that stated, if he ever needed to change his job because of his disability, the government would retrain him for a job in which he could function. He had left World War II without accepting a disability rating that the government had wanted to give him. With his discharge this time came a disability check each month, with his time going back to his first period of service. Too much time had elapsed, and he had lost all educational benefits.

I showed him this letter when he came home that night, and we talked about his going to the Veteran's Administration to see what could be done. He called and made an appointment. When he had his interview, he was asked why he was quitting Shell Chemical. He replied that he was going to school to study for the ministry. The man said he was sorry, that there wasn't anything they could do—Tommy would have to quit because of his disability. Tommy thanked him, turned to leave, and started to open the door when the man called him back. The man said, "Hey, wait a minute, I might be able to help you if you would be willing to take some tests." Tommy readily agreed, and a date was set.

There was a battery of several tests that required three days to complete. When Tommy returned for a decision, the man asked, "Wouldn't you rather be a doctor or a lawyer? There's not much money in preaching."

"I'm not looking for money," Tommy replied.

"Good," answered the man, "that's the answer I was looking for. You see, your tests were so high in the fields of doctor, lawyer, and social worker that we can grant you schooling for any of these fields. I say that you have 'potential that needs developing,' and you can have your schooling under the Rehabilitation Program, which will grant you four years of college, pay for all the books and equipment you will need, plus a living expense check each month. Good luck!"

At first Tommy was so stunned that he did not see the Lord had worked all things out for our good. It had taken those three years in the war, six months in the Korean War, and a disruption in our lives to provide financially for us to secure the necessary education. God always provides for those who wholly and completely follow Him.

God was calling us to sing our song in a new ministry, through the preached Word of God. Not until later did we fully realize that, for those past six years, God had been preparing us for this new step. When Tommy was twelve and I was eight God gave us that song of salvation, that source for beautiful music, and now we could sing: "God Gave the Song!"

3
The Journey

I'm making the journey, Lord,
The greatest journey of all;
My steps may fail, Lord,
So please don't let me fall.

The way is narrow, Lord,
And sometimes I feel alone;
And when my heart fears, Lord,
I softly pray this song:

Give me the heart to be pure;
Give me the faith to be sure,
Give me the strength to endure
All my tribulations.[5]

We are all on a journey, and sometimes the pathway is "narrow and long." At other times we might pass along through sunshine and laughter. I must report that in the years since our complete surrender to God's will for our lives—and our lives changed so drastically—we have not always walked in sunshine and good times. But we all agree that these have been some of the most fulfilling and rewarding days, because God has walked along with us—leading us each step of the way. We have wrapped-up memories, stored away, and sometimes taken out, that we can share when a word or song may remind us of blessings we have experienced along that journey.

Writing of her journey in the solo book that accompanies her album,

"The Way I Feel," Cynthia expresses her feelings with simplicity: "My journey has taken me through smiles and miles, fears and tears, doubt and faith, hope and light. It has been a struggle at times, but struggles sometimes help us grow stronger. My trip through this life has been a time to love and learn. It has been during quiet walks with the Master that I have grown the most."

From January 1953 our way has led through many "fields and forests," and we've climbed many hills, walked through some stony valleys, and stumbled over the jagged rocks, but life has become "sweeter as the days go by."

When we enrolled in the University of Corpus Christi—Tommy as a freshman, I as a senior—new worlds opened for us, but it was more evident in Tommy.

One morning, I was trying to feed the girls, to prepare us for school, and to leave the house in some kind of order. Tommy was sitting at the breakfast table, studying his Greek lesson for the day. He stopped and inquired of me, "Why didn't you tell me it would be like this? There are worlds I never knew existed." Each day unveiled a new discovery. New friendships were made that have lasted a lifetime—we found new places of service for the Lord.

We soon began attending the Greenwood Baptist Church in Aransas Pass where Tommy led the singing, taught the adult Bible class, and I played the piano. It amazes me how the Lord sometimes leads us in seeming circles. Since being in evangelism, we have been able to serve off and on in this same church, now called Second Baptist Church, and we have a close relationship with the people in the community.

Thirty years ago, when we first saw the little church, it was sitting out in the windswept, bleached sand dunes, a poorly-constructed, one-room white building without a porch. The steps led down into the hot sand where you always picked up a shoe full. There was no air-conditioning in the summer and very little heat in the winter. You must travel to the Texas Gulf coast really to experience the heat in the hot, humid summers and the icy wind that blows incessantly off the water in wintertime.

Today there is a lovely brick building with a new educational building where the little white church once stood. When we went back a few years

ago, the educational unit had not been built, and the old church stood
beside the new brick sanctuary.

I had to open those doors and step into that weather-worn house of
worship to feel the memories of yesteryear flood over me. I could envision an old upright piano; one-year-old Patti Jean, sitting in her Taylor-
Tot beside me; Cynthia dangling her short legs from the rough-hewn
homemade bench on the front row, singing with all her might; Tommy
leading the singing, and the congregation, with enraptured faces following along in their old hymn books as they sang God's praises. As I sit
in some magnificent edifice today, surrounded by the trappings of wealth,
I can understand why those humble churches may have often provided
us a deeper worship experience with the Lord.

The congregation consisted mostly of commercial fishermen and their
families, since Aransas Pass is one of the largest fishing villages along the
Texas coast.

A quote from my journal of those days: "We watched many a change
come in that church in the next months, that only God could have
wrought. When we first went there, the people were very poorly dressed,
the children looked as if they had never had a bath, and the men and
women alike used language that would make you flinch every time they
spoke. As the mothers and daddies were converted they began not only
to clean up the outside, but strangely enough, their language became
cleaner. The miracles we saw take place here could even compare to the
miracles of Jesus' day."

The greatest of miracles, salvation, came virtually every time there was
a church service, as people came wanting new life. We saw many lives
transformed by the saving power of our Lord.

Quoting again from my journal (the summer of 1953): "I shall never
forget the day that a hardened ex-convict walked the aisle, not quite
understanding why he was there. Howard (pastor Howard Thrift) asked
Tommy to pray and talk with him, and Brother Howard continued to
plead with the others to come forward. As I was playing the invitation
song and watching Howard, I looked at the man's face and saw the
struggle going on within. Never before had I seen such anguish. His
mother, also having spent time in the penitentiary, but now a new
Christian, had followed him to the altar. She had knelt behind him. With

her tattooed arm, a mark of her former life, she reached out to touch her boy. The minute he surrendered there came a look of release on his face. The hard, calloused face had become soft and peaceful. Never before had I been present when salvation came like that."

Music was an intrinsic part of our life on the college campus. Many times after we had studied all evening, Tommy, Cynthia, and I would gather around the piano to sing, and baby Patti with her "cooing" would make it a quartet.

Our apartment was in an H-shaped barracks that had been converted into living space for the married couples with children. Before we could sing through one song, the back door would open, and our neighbors would begin to join us. Sometimes there were fifteen or twenty people standing around harmonizing and, in fun, trying to outsing the others. This continued to be a practice of ours even when we were in Golden Gate and Southwestern Seminaries.

When we were at Southwestern in Fort Worth, we lived in a house on the hill across the street from Dr. Travis, the pastor of Gambrell Street Baptist Church. One night, hearing the music coming from across the street, he came over to join us. He testified for years that it was one of the finest evenings he had ever spent.

It would be impossible for me to relate all the experiences of the two and a half years we were in college (and that deserves another story), but some stand out as vividly today as thirty years ago. We lived on the waterfront of the campus where we could view all of Corpus Christi Bay. We could look across to the city, strung out in a semicircle around the northwest end of the bay. It was a breathtaking sight, especially at night when the lights turned the whole end of the bay into an exquisite jeweled necklace.

Our few rest times often found us down by the water, either fishing or playing in the sand. Cynthia and her daddy became fishing partners, and many times hauled in enough fish for supper. Patti, just a baby, liked to lie on a blanket and watch the seagulls soar and dip above the water. On the beach Tommy and some of the other preacher boys would gather for long hours, preaching to each other, praying, and singing.

One night his best friend Jack Walker came by. Calling Tommy by the nickname he had picked for him, he yelled from his car, "Didymus, come on, let's go down and pray awhile."

After they left, I put the girls to bed, straightened up around the apartment, and settled down with my preparations for teaching in the primary school on the campus. Since it was late and the boys had not returned, I decided to retire. Sometime around 2 AM, I was awakened with a lusty duet being belted out by Tommy and Jack—"Now I Belong to Jesus." I listened for awhile, but being so tired, I soon fell to sleep and left them singing.

The following morning at the breakfast table, thinking they had been out in front of the house on the beach, I said, "Tommy, you and Jack should have gone on down the road a little farther. I'm sure you kept the whole campus awake."

Looking surprised, he replied. "We did! We were parked down by the bridge. That's almost a quarter of a mile away!"

Out across the bay, the wind and atmosphere had been just right and had carried their voices back across the campus. People still hold them accountable for a lost night of sleep. There's no better way to be awakened than with the singing of praises unto the Lord.

Soon after entering school we heard that Dr. Marko was preaching a revival at First Baptist Church in Alice. It had been over a year since we had seen him, and he had not heard of our decision. One night we gathered the girls and a couple who lived next to us and struck out for Alice, about fifty miles from Corpus. It was a harrowing ride, for about fifteen miles away from the campus, we discovered that the diaper bag had been left behind. Trying not to break any speed laws, we rushed back. While Tommy kept the motor running, I ran in to fetch the bag.

Of course, we were late arriving for the service and couldn't find the nursery, so we carried Patti into the sanctuary with us. Dr. Marko had already begun his message, but when he saw us he stopped, looked quizzically at us, and, in his own inimitable style, announced, "I know that young couple, but the last time I saw them, the young lady was carrying the baby under her heart." It was a thrill to visit with him after the service and update him about the past year—how the Lord had led us and what happiness and satisfaction we now had.

After the meeting that week, Dr. Marko visited with us. Whenever we hear the song, "Does Jesus Care?" a picture returns to us, as he stood beside me at the piano and sang in that glorious high-tenor voice with his delightful accent.

Dr. Marko was a most remarkable man, perhaps the "most unforgettable character" we have ever known. When he graduated from medical school in Vienna, Austria, he also received his doctorate in music at the same time. After coming to America, he sang for a time at the Metropolitan Opera Company in New York. He was converted at age 45, gave up his lucrative medical practice, and surrendered to the ministry shortly afterwards. At the age of 51, he entered Southwestern Seminary, with a young wife and two babies.

After this, and through the years, Tommy lovingly referred to Dr. Marko as his "father in the ministry." Tommy received much help and encouragement from him until his death in the early 1960's. At his passing, Tommy was given the bulk of his library.

The song "Does Jesus Care?" rekindles an old memory forever implanted in our hearts. After spending several months at the church in Aransas Pass, we felt led to resign and return to Corpus, there to attend the Downtown Baptist Church.

For some time the church had considered opening a chapel or Sunday School in the area just south of the drawbridge. Although it was only about eight blocks or so away from the church, the church had been unable to reach the people. The neighborhood was running over with children who wandered around playing in the streets, many of whom went to bed hungry.

For about three blocks leading up to the bridge, there was nothing but beer joints, dives of all kinds, houses of ill-repute, and cheap boarding houses. These people needed a ministry and yet they felt out of place in the Downtown Baptist Church.

Much to our surprise, Tommy was approached by the missions committee about preaching the first Sunday. That first Sunday there were thirty-six present, and after that encouraging attendance the church began to pray about opening a full-time mission. Tommy was asked to become the pastor, and we realized then it was God's plan for our coming to Downtown. Tommy had his first church.

At last—at the age of 29, Tommy would be able to stand behind God's pulpit and preach to the sheep that God had entrusted to His under-shepherd.

It was a very inauspicious beginning, but how excited we were! The church met in a downstairs apartment of a two-story stucco house, with a Mexican family living upstairs.

This proved rather disconcerting at times. Each Sunday morning, just about the time Tommy would begin his sermon, the lady upstairs would begin her washing. The old washing machine must have had one short leg. Besides the noise of the old motor, every time it would go around there would be a loud thump—right over the pulpit. The children of the family and neighborhood would keep marching in and out during the services until Tommy threatened to lock the door. But he knew you never lock a church door on Sunday mornings; folks were simply curious about what was going on inside.

When Tommy gave the invitation on that first Sunday, five-year-old Cynthia climbed down out of her chair, walked up to her daddy, and said, "I want to give my heart to Jesus." I continued to play the invitation song. Tears flowed down my face while the two of them knelt to pray. There was a circle of tears on that old board floor when they arose. She kept saying all afternoon, "I just took one step!" After all, isn't that all we have to do?

On that first Sunday in his first church, there was the first convert, his own first child saved. It seemed to be another of God's stamps of approval on our going through the right door. The next Sunday he baptized little Cynthia, his first baptism.

We soon outgrew that house and moved to a vacant church building where another church had met. We had many varied experiences in the twenty months we were there—some heartwarming, some growing, and some hard times, too. This was not an easy neighborhood to pastor but what a mission field! It wasn't long until the whole community began to respect that "bunch down at the little white church."

It never fails: when a church is actively warring against the devil (and winning in many cases) he does all in his evil power to block the good work. Some in the church had questioned Baptist interpretation of certain doctrines. At a time when we needed reassurance on our stand, the Lord sent a stranger to our door. Could it have been an angel?

It was a summer-like Sunday morning in the spring of that year; the bay looked like a round silver mirror; seagulls called out their morning greetings and broke the stillness of the mirrored water as they dove for their breakfast; and fishermen had put their lines in the water several hours before.

My folks were visiting us that weekend, and Mother and I were late for Sunday School. I had forgotten the diaper bag again. As we parked by the side of the building, a man emerged from his car. His face was drawn to one side, one eye was closed, and he looked as if he were in much pain. He asked in broken English, "Is this a Mexican Baptist church?"

Mother answered, "No, but you certainly would be welcomed. Come on in."

During the Sunday School period we learned his story. He was a Baptist preacher from Los Angeles, on his way to Monterrey, Mexico, there to attend a Fundamental Baptist school. His family had preceded him while he was driving through Texas to visit an uncle in Laredo. Somewhere around Victoria, he had suffered a stroke—hence the paralysis of his face which had caused him to lose sight in one eye.

In the congregation that morning was a young couple who were missionaries to Mexico, home for a visit. They found they had mutual friends with our visitor. Frank the missionary helped translate for him and we were able to piece together his story. Also, Frank knew about the school the man was going to attend.

Just before Tommy pronounced the benediction he spoke to the man, "My brother, I don't know why this thing has happened to you, but I know that God has a reason and as soon as that purpose is fulfilled, He will work out all things for your good."

Turning back to the congregation, Tommy continued, "I think we ought to help our brother along his journey. At least, we can buy him some gas. Mrs. Clawson, would you play something and will the ushers come forward?"

I hurriedly flipped through the hymnal to find a song. It seemed pages fell open to "Does Jesus Care?" and I began softly playing that song. After the ushers returned to the front, Tommy said, "My brother, I want to sing that song for you, for I know Jesus *does* care."

Later, Tommy told us, while he was singing and looking at our visitor, he thought the man was having another stroke, as he grabbed first one eye, then the other, and leaned back in the wooden folding chair. The man reached for Frank's hand and finally came back to a firm position. Tommy averted his eyes and finished singing the song.

As he was about to call for a closing prayer, the man rose and asked, "Brother Preacher, may I say something?"

The man walked up to the platform and turned around. Then, we noticed his face—the paralysis was gone and there was a big smile in its place. Placing his hand over his good eye, he testified, "You know, this morning when I came here, I could not see out of this eye." Taking away his hand, he continued, "But now I can see you—and you—and you!" as he pointed to different ones in the congregation. We had never experienced anything like this before—or since.

A miracle! To whom was it sent?—the injured man or to us who needed a sign from God that we were interpreting His Word correctly? You see, someone had just told us there was no power in a Baptist church. "Does Jesus Care?" Oh, yes, He cares. First Peter 5:7 is so true, "Casting all your care upon him; for he careth for you."

Cynthia's husband, Ragan Courtney, wrote a lyric that Buryl Red set to music, and it became part of their musical *Celebrate Life*. It comes to my mind as I think of God's working in that man's life and ours. I neither remember the man's name nor have we heard of him since, but God spoke to us that day.

He is the wind I soar on;
He is the grass I run through;
He is the one I turn to
When I have to laugh or cry.

He is the sun I sing in;
He is the sea I swim in;
He is the mountain I climb to
When I want to reach a new high.

He is the light of my world;
He is my priceless pearl;

> *He is my answer to why;*
> He is my friend even after I die.
>
> Of all the things He said to me
> The best was:
> Truth will make you free.[6]

In our first pastorate Tommy became known as Brother Tom, and he has been affectionately called that, within and without the church, ever since. He even gets his mail that way at times.

I began calling him "Brother Tom" when we were with our church people because I didn't think they should call him "Tommy." I still refer to him as Brother Tom, and it naturally comes out when I am away from the family. Our two sons-in-law and daughter-in-law also call him that with much love and respect. This seems strange to some. A lady at a club meeting once heard me refer to him like that, and I heard her whisper to another lady, "How odd! I have never heard a woman refer to her husband like that!" That lady would have been even more astonished to hear our oldest grandson ask his Grandpa, "Can I call you Brother Tom?"

During the summer of '83, we took our son Tom's older boy, Nicholas, with us to the General Encampment at Alto Frio, near Leakey, Texas. Brother Tom was the camp pastor for the week. Nicholas, age eight, listened attentively each night and had many questions when we went back to our cabin. On Friday morning Missionary Jim Humphries closed the week with one final invitation for individual commitment to the Lord. Nicholas stepped forward, giving his heart to the Lord.

After lunch, as we were walking back to our cabin for afternoon rest, I said, "You know, Nicholas, I'm your Grandma, but now I'm your sister, also. For you see, when you became a Christian that made us brothers and sisters in Christ."

Brother Tom spoke up and added, "That's why people call me Brother Tom."

Nicholas studied about that for a minute and then asked, "Can I call you Brother Tom?" Then, turning to me with an impish grin, Nicholas added, "And I'll call you Sister Toots!" That's Brother Tom's pet name for me.

Then, thinking a minute longer, Nicholas added, "You know what I'm gonna do? I'm gonna call Daddy and say, 'Hello, Brother Tom, this is Brother Nick!' and this he did by long distance the next morning.

Through the years our journey has carried us to California, to Golden Gate Baptist Theological Seminary, then to Berkeley; to a pastorate on the Monterrey Peninsula; back to Texas and Southwestern Seminary in Fort Worth; and several pastorates in Texas. Like our short time in college, each place is a story unto itself. We were busy making a home and being a family together wherever we stopped.

Our attitude and interpretation of life determine what we will find along the road. A preacher friend once asked Brother Tom where he found the illustrations he uses when preaching. This rather surprised Tom, for his illustrations are mostly taken from our life and the lives of those with whom we have come in contact traveling from church to church.

Music has continued to lead us along. There is a song for every place. In 1951, when we left the Marine Corps and Southern California, we drove away singing, "So Long, It's Been Good to Know You," and four years later we drove back singing, "California, Here We Come . . . right back where we started from . . . open up your Golden Gate" and headed for the seminary in Berkeley.

What an exciting place to be! Being from the coastal plains of Texas, we had never seen cities set on hills, with the houses seemingly stacked one on the other. At night the twinkling of the lights reminded us of fireflies hovering over a lazy bayou back home.

In the spring before Brother Tom graduated, we had purchased a 1955 Ford station wagon, our first new car. At about the same time, we discovered something else new! A baby was on the way. That meant I would not be able to teach that year, since the baby was due in January.

From the first time we laid eyes on the Oakland Bay Bridge, tying those hill-crested cities together, we were enamoured by the area, especially San Francisco. We never seemed to absorb enough of that resplendent city set high on the hill, like a sentinel guarding the entrance to the surrounding cities and villages. We made several sightseeing trips on Saturdays, when we could all be together after the school week, and delighted in driving up and down those steep hills.

But one trip was not much fun. . . .

After receiving his B.A. degree under the Government Rehabilitation Program for disabled veterans, Brother Tom was to be given one year in the seminary under the GI Bill of Rights for his duty in the Korean War. When the first check of the school year did not arrive, we drove to San Francisco to the VA office, to see what could be done. The next two months came and went—still no check. Finally, after many trips to the VA office, the problem was turned over to the Veterans of Foreign Wars office (VFW). They discovered that some clerk, in sending the papers from the San Antonio office in Texas to San Francisco, had changed one word. Under the section called "Designation," the word "Clergyman" had been changed to "Minister." The clerk, apparently not knowing the words are synonymous, had written: "Change of Designation," denying Tom continuance of his monthly check.

After making a 2,500-mile move from Corpus Christi to Berkeley, enrolling in the seminary, landing a job, locating a place to live that we could afford, finding a doctor for the time left in my pregnancy, and with no monthly check coming from the government, we decided that we must sell something. Alas, the car would have to go!

When the mistake was found, the Veterans Administration issued a check for back payments, and the monthly checks began to come. But by that time, we could not save the car.

So, one foggy, misty day we drove to San Francisco where we delivered the car to a repossession garage. The four of us sadly turned and walked away.

At the corner we boarded a cable car and started down the hill into Chinatown. There we sat on the outside bench with our feet dangling off the side. Yours truly, eight months pregnant, with tears flowing down her face; Brother Tom with his arm around my shoulders; the little girls sitting like bewildered kittens, looking up at us and not fully understanding why we were not still riding in our blue station wagon. I was grateful for the ever-present, misty rain and hoped that perhaps our fellow passengers would attribute my tears to the rain.

We aimlessly wandered through the shops in Chinatown, looking at the unusual gifts, smelling the strange odors, seeing with eyes that had no heart behind them. For a long time we had promised ourselves a trip to Chinatown, but we were too heartsick to enjoy any of it. Leaving there, we walked toward the heart of downtown, stopping long enough to eat a bite of lunch. We then rode a bus to the station where we caught the F-train to Berkeley, where an old secondhand car awaited us.

For us the Golden Gate had turned to brass.

We had rented an upstairs flat a few blocks from the seminary and only two blocks from the nearest elementary school. Patti had trouble understanding why she couldn't go to school too, because she had spent the first three years of her life in nursery school at college.

One day Patti and I were standing in the front yard waiting for Cynthia to come home from school. The usual fog had blanketed the city, and you could see only about a block down the street. As we watched our little second grader skipping down the street, singing at the top of her voice, I knew that, although it might be foggy, there was sunshine in her heart. She called out, "Mother, I have a song I want to show you."

As she came to a halt in front of me, I replied, "*Show* me a song!"

She caught her breath, began to sing, and, putting in all the motions to her song, she sang:

> You put your right hand in,
> You put your left hand out,
> You put your right hand in
> And shake it all about.
> You do the hokey pokey
> And you turn yourself around
> That's what it's all about.7

When she finished, I smiled and asked, "Cynthia, do you know what you're doing?"

Hanging her head, she quietly admitted, "Yes, Ma'am, I'm dancing."

Smiling at her, I replied, "Well, I think you had better *show* your daddy your song when he comes home."

When Brother Tom visited the teacher and explained that we would rather Cynthia not be in the dancing class, the teacher was quite puzzled, not understanding about Baptist seminary students. At that time, dancing to Baptists was akin to drinking, smoking, and gambling.

"Well, what will I do with her?" the teacher asked.

"Just give her a book to read or something, but I don't want her taking dancing lessons."

There were other children from the student body of the seminary, and I don't think the teachers and principal had ever encountered that kind of situation. Since Baptist work in California in the early 1950's was still in the pioneer stages, we were acutely aware that Baptists and other Christians needed to take a stand on Christian conduct.

A month later, we moved across the mountain to Walnut Creek, a quiet little town nestled in a verdant valley. It was here that our son, Tommy, Jr., was born.

When we came home from the hospital, Brother Tom held the baby in his arms and said, "Hello, there, my Tommy Boy," and the nickname stuck. The girls shortened it to "Tombo," and the family and close friends of his growing-up years still refer to him as Tombo.

While in high school he later asked me, "Mother, please don't call me Tombo when you come to the school. I don't mind you and Daddy and the church people calling me that, but just call me Tommy when you're around my school friends." I guess they had teased him about it. We really tried, but by that time the name was ingrained into the family, so I'm afraid we didn't always make it.

Our stay in California was for only two years. We felt so certain it was God's will for us to be there, to attend Golden Gate and also to live with and learn about the people to whom we would minister the rest of our lives, we thought. So we were distressed when trouble arose in our first church. Because of our own immaturity in the ministry and misunderstanding some well-meaning folk, we looked back to the "holy land"—Texas—and wanted to go home. Thinking *nobody loves us—everybody hates us,* we left California in June of 1957 with no song in our hearts.

Shortly after we arrived in Houston, Brother Tom was called as associate pastor to our home church, Broadway Baptist Temple, where he had surrendered to the ministry and been licensed to preach—where "family" was. "I Love Those Dear Hearts and Gentle People . . . who live in my hometown." Our friends, who could not possibly know the awfulness we felt upon realizing that we had run away from the Lord's will for our lives, reached out to us, put their arms of love about us, ministered to our hearts, and in turn let us minister to them.

Brother M. T. Jenkins, the pastor, shared his pulpit with Brother Tom. Brother Jenkins was gracious and loving. The two preachers even bought suits alike one time, because they both liked that particular cut and style. They also decided to buy ties alike simply to have a good laugh. The laugh was on them—even though they sat side by side on the platform, no one noticed or commented on the suits!

We were encouraged and sustained by everyone's love in the months that followed, as only our Christian family can do.

> Blest be the tie that binds
> Our hearts in Christian love;
> The fellowship of kindred minds
> Is like to that above.
> —John Fawcett

In reflection, we realize that the family of God in California loved as much as the family of God in Texas, but it required maturing on our part to understand it.

One privilege of God's ministry is getting to meet so many of the Family, but we must admit that as in any family, certain members are drawn to one another. Yes, we do have some favorite people and some favorite places.

For instance, the hill country around Leakey is one of our favorite parts of Texas, and over the years its people have assumed their place close to the top of our list.

At Leakey there is one of the oldest Baptist encampment grounds in Texas. We first visited there in 1959 when we led a caravan of cars, loaded with giggly little girls from First Baptist Church, Pleasanton, where Brother Tom served as associate pastor and educational director. The little GA (Girl's Auxiliary) members were anticipating the coming week—a whole week they could be away from home, a week they could make their own decisions and play grown-up. Cynthia was eleven, and it was only the second time for her to be away from us that long.

On Friday, we returned to pick up the girls. When we drove onto the campground, we could see Cynthia in front of the tabernacle, as she played and laughed with the other girls. We gave our familiar toot on the car horn. Seeing us, she began to run and started to cry. The nearer she came, the harder she cried. With arms wide open, we ran to meet her, afraid that something terrible was wrong. We asked, "Honey, what's the matter? Are you all right? Did someone hurt your feelings?"

Shaking all over and struggling to gain control, she gasped out, "No, I'm just so glad to see you! I've been so homesick!" We assured her we had been homesick for her, too. We didn't like for our family to be apart.

That year she came away with a *new song,* "His Way Mine" by Dick and Bo Baker, and a *new committal* in her heart that this would be true of her life. Already, she was stretching forth, searching for God's will for her life.

> God has a place for ev'ry planned creation,
> A path for ev'ry star to go,
> He drew the course for ev'ry river's journey,
> Now I know He has a way for me.[8]

This first visit began a "love affair" for all of us with Alto Frio Baptist Encampment and the town of Leakey. Since we grew up on the coastal plains of Texas, anytime we see a mound of dirt that could be called a "hill," we become excited. Whenever we approach the area around Austin, New Braunfels, or San Antonio, we all begin to sit up a little straighter and start "oohing" and "aahing" at the scenes of the splendid hill country. Usually one of us starts singing "The Hills of Home," and we all join in with gusto. Somehow we seem to feel a little closer to God out in the hills.

We leave San Antonio. For several miles we travel in a lovely valley, rich in grain and pastureland; then, at Sabinal, we make our turn towards the blue hills, in which flows the ice-cold Frio River that meanders down through the canyon bearing the same name. Crossing the river at Concan, we turn up into the canyon, and every time we do, we get a little light-headed, not from the altitude, but from the joy of being back in the Frio Canyon. At the southern end of the canyon is Garner State Park, a favorite camping and picnicking place in this part of Texas. Along the river camps nestle in among the cypress, oak, and cedar trees. Several thousand people make their way there each summer. Many of them buy their own places after a summer or two and return to live out their retirement days.

Leakey is a typical West Texas ranching town, set amid some of the most magnificent scenery in the hill country. It flourishes in the summer, but goes to sleep in the winter, as the summer guests pack up and return to the cities from which they came. It wakes for a short time in winter during the hunting season.

Our lives soon became intertwined with the First Baptist Church there, and it's sort of a "homecoming" when we get a chance to visit or serve there. Brother Tom has held several revivals there.

When Tombo graduated from high school in 1974, he was called as summer music and youth director, and among his responsibilities, he and the pastor, Harvey Hulse, served in the resort ministry along the river. They held regular Sunday morning services in several camps before the Sunday School hour at the church. Tombo would play his guitar and sing—then Harvey would preach.

The church found Tombo a quaint little rock cabin on the campgrounds for him to use during the summer. It overlooked the turn of the Frio River as it flows by the camp. He almost could have jumped from his front step into the river.

Since this was his first time away from home, it was exciting to him. In a letter he shared with us what it's like when an eighteen-year-old boy leaves home for the first time: "I just finished taking my afternoon dip in the cool Frio River. The pounding (country term meaning to provide groceries and household items for a church staff member) the church gave me was really great. None of the kids were there, but it was OK. I got all sorts of canned goods, preserves and jellies, squash and onions, cola, and pizza and spaghetti. The pizza and spaghetti are the kind where you make the dough and all. Last night for supper, I had the spaghetti and meat sauce with Parmesan cheese on top, and that wonderful cola. It turned out pretty good except I didn't have any salt to add to it, but it was still good. Also, at the pounding the ladies made cookies, so I got to bring home a plate. In fact, I'm eating some right now. My bed here is awfully uncomfortable, because it makes me sweat a lot. It's got a plastic cover over the mattress, and no air can get in or out. But that's just one of the difficulties I have to go through when I'm batchin.' " And he liked it enough to return a couple of summers later when they called him.

After that first sight of the canyon, we wanted to have a "retreat" of our own. In the summer of 1973 we were able to purchase twenty acres on a ranch that had been subdivided for smaller plots. We finally landed our own "Hill," a desire planted in our hearts when we first gazed on those hills of California.

That "Hill" was just what we had been looking for. When Brother Tom's mother asked what we could grow on it, I replied, "Rocks, I guess." We did have a couple of acres down in a little meadow before the land began to rise up the hill and probably could have planted a small garden where an old cattle pen once had stood. The ground was rich and fertile there, but we didn't want to plant a garden; we just wanted to sit and look at our "mountain." We thought of many enchanting names we might call our little ranch—like the one we had seen in California, named "No Tengo Rancho" (translation: I have no ranch.), but no name ever stuck. It was just "the hill."

We enjoyed our hill for several years, but when the Lord led us into evangelism and we left San Antonio, he gave us a lovely home on a small private lake outside Conroe. We realized then that the hill would probably never be our retirement home. It soon became a too-expensive plaything, 350 miles away; so, in the third year of evangelism we sold it to stay in evangelism another year. It was a dream that we held onto for a little while, and we stored up many pleasant memories for the whole family.

The Frio River is one of four rivers, including the Nueces, Sabinal, and Medina Rivers, that form deep canyons for miles. Some of these miles are parallel to each other as they flow toward the Gulf of Mexico.

As we meet people and make friends, some of us are naturally attracted to others who have the same likes and dislikes. Music has been the magnetic force which has initially drawn us to many who have become some of our dearest friends. Friends are such a blessing from God. We have far too many to mention them all, but when we think of our preaching ministry and music—there is Merle "Skinney" Dodd.

Because his physique and Brother Tom's were similar when they met—rather rotund—Brother Tom enjoyed introducing them as "Tweedle Dee" and "Tweedle Dum." With the passing of years they have become more portly, so he now refers to them as "Tweedle Dum" and "Tweedle Dummer."

Merle has a used car lot and junkyard in Houston, secondary to his mission for the Lord. Many times he has simply shut the operation down if he couldn't find someone to run it for him while he went to a revival or some other place of witnessing. Brother Tom delights in calling him "a junkie for the Lord."

We go back twenty years when Brother Tom was invited to conduct a revival in Terre Haute, Indiana. Talking to one of the deacons, Tom mentioned the need of a singer to go with us. The deacon quickly answered, "Why don't you take Skinney Dodd with you?"

"Can he sing?" asked Brother Tom. He had met Merle and found him to be a fine Christian but had never heard him sing.

"Sure," replied the deacon.

That night after supper, Brother Tom announced to me that he had invited Merle to go with us. I was horrified and asked, "Can he sing?"

"Johnny (the deacon) said he could," he assured me.

"But," I stammered, "what if he *can't* sing, and what if he isn't a good traveler? After all, we've got to be on the road for two weeks, and you want us to travel with someone we don't know!"

Brother Tom answered, "Well, I guess we'll find out."

That was the start of a continuing ministry that has carried us from that first revival in Terre Haute to Chicago, to Houston, to San Antonio, and even to the Hawaiian Islands.

We found that Merle could sing (and he is a great traveling companion), and how he blesses our hearts with his clear, melodic tenor voice! But that's not the greatest facet about Merle Dodd. His sweet spirit, his desire to witness, and his love for Jesus and people are obvious in all he does.

For instance, in Terre Haute the morning after we arrived, Merle told the pastor to give him a list of people who needed visiting. With his list he walked out the door. That night we found he had taken a map of Terre Haute and had either walked or ridden the city bus until he had finished his list. In San Gabriel, Texas, he was on his own during the day, and he helped the farmers feed their cattle. He even fed the catfish in one big pond on the farm where he was staying. We have gone together to Braidwood, Illinois, several times. The one time we went without him, the people of the church laughingly suggested that we not come back without Merle. He always endears himself to the hearts of the people.

His equally dedicated wife, Wanda, has been a part of the team on many occasions. Though not a singer like Merle, her openness and genuine Christian love minister in numerous ways.

In the fall of 1978 we were asked by the Home Mission Board of our denomination if we would consider and pray about going to Hawaii in the spring to participate in the "Living Proof Crusade" to be held in the islands. The Board suggested if we could enlist a singer, we would have our team complete and would be assigned to a church. We immediately thought of Merle and Wanda and called them. They readily agreed they would go with us. The one stipulation was we would have to pay our own way; the church to which we were assigned would take care of us while we were there.

We were assigned to the First Southern Baptist Church in Ewa Beach. On arrival in Honolulu we were warmly received with the traditional welcome by the pastor, Bill Sanders, and his wife Annie, as they placed the floral leis around our necks.

At Bill's suggestion, and after having to tie and untie our shoes each time we visited in a home, we soon bought thong sandals for our feet and aloha shirts for Brother Tom and Merle.

As always, Merle made a hit with the choir members. He felt right at home, so much so that one night we walked in during choir practice to see him on the platform devoid of his thongs, as barefooted as any native. He laughed and explained that the little piece between his toes made them hurt. He did put them on for the service!

In this church were some of the most vibrant, attractive young people we have ever met. Many of them who had just left the drug scene were actively telling others what Jesus had done for them. One night during the meeting, three young college-aged men sang a song that one of them, Kamalei Mark Tewes, had written with the typical island beat:

I like bananas
I know that mangoes are sweet
I like papayas,
But nothing can beat
The sweet, sweet love of God. . . .[9]

Time arrived for us to bid "aloha" and return to the mainland. We left with heavy hearts because in such a short time we had grown to love those marvelous people. The young people cut their classes in school that last morning (they spent many hours the night before making leis for us) to meet us at the airport and give us an aloha send-off. One young man had made a lei for my head. He put it on me and said, "This is a crown for you." That crown could be exceeded only by the one the Lord will give us.

Our last sight there was this group of lovely Christian young people, with Mark and his guitar leading them in singing, "I like bananas."

Two years later, Ragan and Cynthia went to Hawaii with the young people from the First Baptist Church of Dallas. There they conducted concerts and witnessed along the beaches. When they were visiting us after their trip, Cynthia was changing the baby's diaper and singing softly to him, "I like bananas, I like papayas . . ." and I began singing with her. She asked, "How do you know that song?" I told her about Mark and the other young people at Ewa Beach, and she exulted, "Well, they're singing that song all over Hawaii."

In October, 1982, we had a brief word from Mark, and I want to quote it in its entirety: "Aloha, just thought I'd drop a note to ask your prayer for revival to be done at Thanksgiving on Molokai. You did a revival at Ewa Beach and God spoke to my heart about evangelism. I know God is going to use me mightily to draw people to Himself. Thanks for loving Him—Godspeed." Mark.

Our paths touch, we journey on miles apart, and yet the tie of Jesus binds us together forever. So many friends have ministered to us through words and music (full-time or otherwise), and have indelibly stamped themselves on our lives. For each of them we give thanks unto the Father. After pastoring for twenty-four years, the Lord opened still another door, and we really began to "journey." For nine years, Brother

Tom had pastored the Hot Wells Baptist Church in San Antonio, when in the spring of 1976, he felt led to resign and enter into full-time evangelism.

Our journey the last eight years has taken us from Florida to Hawaii, from Chicago and Erie, Pennsylvania, to the Texas valley, and points in between. We have had the excitement of those early years in the ministry; of depending wholly on the Lord; of being used of Him in so many ways and different places.

"The Family of God" has come to mean much more to us as we have seen the circle enlarge, and we have realized that we have a "ready-made family" wherever we go. It is always sad when we reach the closing service with a particular church and have to say "good-bye," knowing that we may not see some of our new brothers and sisters again until our journey is finished. But what a victorious choir we will be able to sing in: no off-key voices—we will all sing on perfect pitch; no bashful heads —we will all have perfect confidence in Christ, each taking his or her place of best service. Someone has estimated there will be one hundred million voices in that heavenly choir. In Revelation 5:9 it says, "And they sung a new song" (See Rev. 5:8-12). God gives us a song for this life, and He will give us a new song forever and forever.

Brother Tom has always insisted that he wants to be able to sing a duet with David, the sweet singer of Israel.

"His Music" has led us, has encouraged us, has sustained us in times of tiredness and troubles. It has brought joy to our hearts. It is the chord of music that has truly bound us together as a family.

Cynthia sings a song, "His Music," by her friend George Gagliardi that speaks to us when we think about music:

> I look to Jesus and hear His music,
> His music is the truest love song ever sung.
> It's for everyone
> All children old and young.
> And if I reach a hundred I know there will be
> No other melody
> That's like the one He sings to me.[10]

4
La Familia de Dios
(The Family of God)

I'm so glad I'm a part of the family of God,
I've been washed in the fountain,
Cleansed by His Blood!
Joint heirs with Jesus as we travel this sod
For I'm part of the family of God.[11]

English-speaking Christians traveling in foreign countries have discovered the only words they generally can understand in a sermon— "Amen" and "Hallelujah." In the singing of hymns it is an entirely different story. Though the words sound strange, the tune is many times a familiar one and the language barrier is broken down as music helps to consummate worship.

Brother Tom recalls how in 1945 in Tsingtao, China, he wandered onto the porch of a Chinese Christian church. At this time he was backslidden and away from God. Standing there on the porch, hearing familiar Christian tunes, was more than he could stand. He turned and walked away with the hymns and the conviction they brought still ringing in his ears.

Longfellow wrote: "Music is the universal language of mankind."

Countless times through the years the language barrier has been overcome by music. I remember in the early days of our marriage, we spent a delightful Sunday afternoon with two young men from South America, when music proved to be the cementing bond between our differing cultures.

Our church was near the harbor area of Houston, and it was not uncommon to see foreign sailors passing by en route to town. That particular Sunday morning, coming from Sunday School, we stopped to visit with some friends. As we stood on the sidewalk, two neatly dressed young men in khaki suits approached us and asked, "Que oras son?" Tommy, trying desperately to recall his high-school Spanish, held out his arm and let them look at his watch.

They thanked him. Instead of walking down the street, they stood looking curiously at the church building. I must say the building was not the typical one with stained-glass windows and a spire on top. We were constructing our church plant by sections and that building would one day be the educational plant.

Instinctively feeling their loneliness, Tommy explained in his inadequate Spanish that this was a church and invited them to worship with us. During the song service, one of the young men enthusiastically joined in the singing, wanting to practice *his* high school English. Tommy held his book with him and tried to point to the words. The other boy smiled and seemed to be keeping time with the music. They were both respectful and joined in during the prayer time. During the sermon the young man with his limited knowledge of English tried to listen as best he could. The other boy dozed.

Following the service, we impulsively invited them home for lunch. We also invited Tommy's sister, Lois Ruth, who was studying Spanish at that time, thinking she might be of help.

Our transportation was a company pickup truck, so loading the boys into the back of the truck, we headed home, apprehensively asking each other, "How are we going to talk to them?"

As we sat around the table, it wasn't as difficult as we had anticipated. We talked by sign language, by pointing to objects on the table, saying the word in English and then it repeating in Spanish. We all laughed at the feeble attempts we made in saying each word, and a bond of friendship began to occur among the four of us.

The real thrill followed lunch as I played the piano and everyone gathered around and began to harmonize. After singing through several popular and classical numbers, I then began to play "Ave Maria." At this point the young man who knew no English excitedly began gesturing for the others to be quiet. He then sang the Latin solo in a rich, full tenor voice, smiling from ear to ear, proud that finally here was a song *he* knew. He could share his gift of song with us. It was still another language, apart from English or Spanish, that became a bridge of communication for us that day. There is no language barrier in music.

Late that afternoon we reluctantly returned them to their ship. For many years, each Christmas brought greetings from South America. The mother of one boy wrote, thanking us for taking care of her son while he was in a strange land, and those pleasant moments were recalled when music had helped to span the bridge between our two cultures.

Music can carry us around the world with just one song.

"Around the World in Eighty Days," a popular theme from a movie by the same name in the late 1950s, would carry a mother and two little girls far more miles than the ten miles they drove to school each day. Living in Houston at that time, I was teaching the fourth grade at the Second Baptist Church elementary school, then located at the edge of downtown Houston. Cynthia was in my fourth grade class and Patti, in kindergarten.

Driving down the freeway each morning, we would sing, "Around the world I've searched for you. . . ." and we would be transported to other worlds as if on a magic carpet. The traffic became less of a hassle as we glided through, oblivious to the roar and congestion of the cars. We were free—through music we could fly "around the world."

The world is not so large, as was proved four years ago when Cynthia and Ragan joined the Second Baptist Church of Houston as "Artists in Residence" and some remembered her as that little fourth-grade girl. The doctor who had ushered her into the world, Dr. Ed Crocker, put his arm around her and proudly announced, "I got to spank her first."

Many years after we sang that song, Cynthia made that trip around the world. In 1970 she flew around the world with Billy Hanks's evangelism team. The first few stops along the trip were Tokyo, Taiwan, and Hong Kong.

One night in San Antonio, we received a telephone call from a friend, Gwen Hall, who asked, "Do you know where your daughter is?"

"Well," I replied, "I guess she's in Hong Kong," hastily checking her itinerary pasted on the bulletin board by the phone.

Gwen replied, "No, I believe she's in Saigon."

Letting out a squeal, I said, "Well, she'd better not be—there's a war going on over there!"

Then Gwen began telling us that her husband, Darrell, had just called from Vietnam "by way of Mars" and asked, "Guess who I had lunch with today? A beautiful redhead, Cynthia Clawson!"

Major Darrell Hall had just left Brooks Aerospace Medical Center in San Antonio to begin a tour in Vietnam as chaplain at Bien Hora Air Base, and it was his first Sunday there. As he sat on the front row of the chapel, he couldn't believe his eyes. There Cynthia sat on the platform.

The evangelistic team had been asked to fly from Hong Kong for the Sunday service and to sing for the servicemen. The speaker for the morning was Dr. S. M. Lockridge from Los Angeles. After the service the three of them had lunch together. Halfway around the world music drew old friends together.

A few weeks later, Brother Tom received a call from a lady who reported that her husband had been in the service that Sunday in Vietnam. Because the girl who sang was from San Antonio, too, he had taped the song and sent it to his wife. The thoughtful lady sent us a copy. As we later listened to the tape, it was rather scary to think of Cynthia being over there, for as she was singing "How Great Thou Art," we could hear the roar of the planes as they flew overhead. But the Lord always cares for His own, even though they may be 10,000 miles away from home and in the middle of a war.

From Hong Kong to India for four weeks, and on to Holland with a short stopover in Greece—"around the world," not in eighty days but in seventy-five—singing God's song.

Music knows no boundaries!

A couple of years ago when Brother Tom was in a revival at the First Baptist Church of Aspermont, Texas, a lady from India asked, "Do you have a daughter named Cynthia?"

"Yes, I do," replied Brother Tom.

She exclaimed, "I thought about Cynthia when I saw your name on a poster advertising the meeting. When she was in India, I was her convenor (translator) in her meetings. How she blessed our hearts! I shall never forget that lovely singing and the beautiful spirit she had."

The language may be different, but music touches almost every person's heart and evokes a response when words fail. Sometimes though, the response is not what we expect. A few years ago, Brother Tom visited a church in Houston where Evangelist Jerry Young was preaching. Jerry invited him to sing.

Brother Tom had been practicing his Spanish, learning a few new songs he might use if the occasion arose. He had bought two books in Spanish: a hymnal and a book of Bill Gaither's.

That night as he sang a medley on the "Family of God," he noticed one Hispanic family present. As he was singing the song, he quickly decided to test his Spanish, shifting to "La Familia de Dios" on the second chorus. The family responded by immediately sitting up straighter, smiling, and nodding their heads. But coldness and a stiffening of backs crept over the rest of the congregation, smiles faded and the people simply sat there—no "amens" afterwards.

Later, Brother Tom found out that the church had undergone trouble over the "tongues" issue, and the people that night thought he had broken loose with an "unknown tongue."

Through the piano Patti was able to cross over the language barrier when we first moved to San Antonio to pastor the Hot Wells Baptist church. She was asked by the missions committee to play the piano for the Sunday worship services in our Hispanic mission. She was honored to be asked and readily accepted. After the first Sunday, we asked her how she liked it. Her answer? "Fine, but I'm going to have to learn to play the piano in Spanish!" And that she did. Translating from English to Spanish often causes the rhythm of the song to change somewhat, and you do have to play *in* Spanish.

Patti quickly made friends with one of the young women her age, as they taught the children in Sunday School, and they began singing together in both English and Spanish. They were asked to sing at several places other than the mission. "Ahora Soy de Cristo"—"Now I Belong to Jesus"—was one of the first songs Patti sang in Spanish.

Shortly after our move to San Antonio we shared our church choir with the Chinese Baptist Church. We were invited to sing for the Wednesday evening service. The ladies of the church served refreshments afterwards so we could all get acquainted. There was much smiling and bowing while some of the younger members translated for the older members and for us. As a part of a Christian family, we shared a bond with each other in spite of the faulty English and Chinese.

Another time music reached out to cross not a language barrier, but a cultural line, was when Cynthia and Myrtle Hall, a black vocalist well-known for her work with Billy Graham, shared a concert at Prairie View A & M University, a black school near Houston.

The audience was attentive and seemed to enjoy hearing both women as they sang, but afterwards Myrtle, putting her arm around Cynthia, remarked, "You know, I think you got across to the audience with your soul-type music better than I did with my style." Cynthia felt that this was a genuine compliment. The late Arthur Godfrey once observed, when Cynthia was appearing on the *All-American College Show,* "The beauty of this girl is, she has real soul."

Thinking about Prairie View College reminds me of a pleasant Sunday we spent in Jewett, Texas, when Cynthia was about thirteen, Patti nine, and Tombo five. We had been invited to have lunch and attend the afternoon service with our neighboring church, St. John Baptist Church, a black congregation. It was an all-day celebration of their lodge. We were one of three white families invited; we felt honored and had looked forward to that Sunday. It was the children's first experience in a black church, and they were wide-eyed as we drove up in front of the little white building.

Lunch was spread on tables out under the oak trees, and we were royally fed. Tombo, with his lunch plate, straddled the trunk of a fallen tree. It was just the right height for him. On the other end sat a cute black boy about his age, all dressed up in a suit with bow tie and all. He was sitting with his plate in front of him, silently watching Tombo. Neither boy spoke a word, but as they ate, they began scooting nearer each other. As the last bite was taken the little boy jumped up, running behind the nearest tree. Tombo followed him. Only he ran to the other side of the tree.

We watched them as they played their game of "hide and seek" around the tree, not one word passing from one to the other. It soon was time to go in for the singing, so the game came to a halt.

The black choir took its place with the director or "starter" positioned to the left of his choir. Such singing as we had never heard emanated from that small group. An old favorite of ours, "Leaning on the Everlasting Arms," was rendered as only a black choir can sing it. I watched the girls' faces light up and their lips move in perfect tempo with the choir.

On the way home, we asked the children about their impressions of the afternoon. What had they liked most?

Patti, speaking up first, commented, "I really liked the singing and all those amens. Our people ought to amen you like that, Daddy."

Cynthia added, "You know, after hearing that wonderful singing, it's a good thing they didn't give an invitation—I might have moved my membership."

And Tombo, not to be outdone by his big sisters, piped up, "I sure did like that little Mexican boy!"

What a lesson to be learned here—with children there is no barrier, language or cultural. We are all a part of the "La Familia de Dios" in Christ.

On the Texas-Mexico border, in a giant bend of the Rio Grande, lie stony mountain towers looming over the dry, sunbaked desert below. If you could drop a plumb line due south of the Carlsbad Caverns in New Mexico to the Rio Grande in Texas, west of this line you will find ninety mountain peaks over a mile high. The land is desolate, bold, rough, and lonely, but those who can see God's handiwork in the vast desert waste will stand awestricken before the grandeur of the place.

Its inhabitants, some 1,500 to 2,000 people in an area covering more than 5,000 square miles, plus some 1,100 square miles in the Big Bend National Park area—are like the land, the last of the great American frontiersmen. But what a mission field! Individualists in a time when it is fashionable to conform; those who have left behind the "plastic world"; retirees who have rejected city living; the ever-present "wetbacks" who wade across the river, always watchful for the Border Patrol, who try to protect an impossible border line; outlaws; and renegades.

One of our friends whose family has lived on the Terlingua Ranch for several years laughingly declared, with pride in his voice, "We're all misfits in society, or we wouldn't be here!"

In the midst of this modern-day mission field stands a little white church perched on a slight hill beside the highway leading from Alpine to the Big Bend National Park. Big Bend Baptist Church, like a beacon in a lighthouse, can be seen for some seven miles as you approach it from the north.

It has been our privilege for the past four years to be there either in revival or Bible study. In 1984 we took Patti and our little four-year-old grandson, Matthew, with us. On the first Sunday night she gave a mini-concert and sang two songs everyone could relate to in those mountains around us: "How Big Is God?" and "How Great Thou Art."

> Oh Lord my God! When I in awesome wonder
> Consider all the worlds thy hands have made,
> I see the stars, I hear the rolling thunder,
> Thy pow'r thro'out the universe displayed,
> ....
> Then sings my soul, my Savior God to thee;
> How great thou art, how great thou art![12]

Each night she sang and played the piano before her daddy preached, and again on Saturday night she gave a full concert.

And what would the wild West be without a stage stop? Just a couple of miles north of the church, there is the only mini-mart and gas stop for seventy miles, run by a young couple new to the community. After the concert on Saturday night, with about half of the congregation we made our way there for fellowship and to make them feel welcomed in Big Bend.

The building is not the typical drive-in type, for it is more like a living room with counters laden with food down at one end of the room. There is a big fireplace covering the entire north wall with bookshelves on each side. Here is displayed an impressive collection of rocks, books to be lent, and chairs in front for "settin' a spell." Our host and hostess made bite-sized roast beef sandwiches, and we were served cold drinks from the ice chest.

In that group was the Juan Grandos family from Santa Elena, Mexico, who had recently moved across the Rio Grande to work on the Texas side. Juan speaks fair English, the children speak a little better, but Mama Rose speaks none. As we gathered around the one guitar we had, they endeavored to join in. Then the guitar was passed to Juan, and he and his family serenaded the rest of us with Spanish hymns. Later I noticed Patti had joined the group, kneeling down beside Rose to share her Spanish hymnal. Patti seemed right at home, and it made Rose feel comfortable.

Next morning, when the invitation was given at the close of the worship service, the Grandos family (all eight of them) joined the church. The pastor is hoping to use Juan as the leader of a Spanish department so other Hispanics in that area can be reached for the Lord.

Ever since the church's beginning, they have not only tried to reach the people in the Big Bend area but have been a part of the river ministry, reaching over the river to carry medical supplies, food, clothing, and Christ.

At the close of the evening service, Patti sang two songs relative to the area and the faithful workers for the Lord at Big Bend Baptist Church. As she introduced the first one, she said, "We are so close to the Rio Grande, the only water anywhere around here, and wouldn't it be foolish if we took the water that we drink and poured it into the river? Just so, when we witness only to each other and those around us, and don't take the Water to those who are dying for a drink of the Living Water, we are wrong. There is a song that Cynthia sings in one of her albums, "Stop This Haulin' Water to the Sea" written by Reba Rambo and Donny McGuire. It goes:

> See the fields so dry and thirsty
> They're dying from a lack of rain;
> And here I'm standing in the fountain,
> Watching them perish,
> And who's to blame?
>
> I'm gonna carry the water to the desert;
> Stop this haulin' water to the sea!
> I'm gonna seek out the dry and barren places—
> The sick ones need the doctor!
> I'm gonna stop this haulin' water to the sea![13]

And then Patti softly began to sing:

"Que en mi puedan ver a Jesus,"
(Let others see Jesus in you)

Que en mi puedan ver a Jesus,
(Let others see Jesus in you)

Contando la historia De su gran amor,
(Keep telling the story, be faithful
    and true)

Que en mi puedan ver a Jesus.
(Let others see Jesus in you.)[14]

What a fitting way to close a week's revival where only a river divided two worlds, and yet in Christ there is no division, no language barrier, no cultural line, and we're all a part of "La Familia de Deos.

5

I Don't Have to Wait

I don't have to wait until I'm grown up,
To be loving and true;
There are many little deeds of kindness
That each day I can do.

I can read my Bible and pray,
Be a loving helper alway;
I don't have to wait until I'm grown up,
To be what Jesus wants me to be.[15]

Once a wall poster hanging in the girls' room read:

A bird sings
not because he has all the answers
but because he has a song!

Children are born with a song, the desire to express their joy of living, to imitate the sounds they hear about them—the birds and animals of nature, the mechanical sounds that man has produced. But often this song dies before it is full-grown because there is no one to help them develop their gift. Oh, I know not all people are born with a melodious sound, one pleasing to the ear, but the song of the soul should not be repressed. Every person does have a song.

As parents, we should help our children develop the gifts they have. What a stirring picture to see a young mother, cradling her tiny babe and singing "Rock-a-Bye Baby in the Tree Top." Her tune may not come out with the clearest tonal sounds, but in her heart she is expressing love and a wonder of God's gift—her offspring. The infant feels the warmth of the mother's love and the contentment in music, however feebly it might be presented.

Even though it may later become evident that the child has no special gift in music, he can be given the opportunity of listening to great music and participating in musical activities. Then he will be able to carry a song in his heart.

An old wives' tale goes that if a mother sings a lot while she is carrying her baby in the womb, the baby will be musical. When I first heard this some thirty-five years ago, I laughed and quipped, "Oh, sure." But there may be some truth in this statement, according to the latest findings in prenatal care of the infant.

An article in the *Reader's Digest* (December 1983) recently asked the question, "What Do Babies Know?" A portion of one paragraph states: "The baby's ears function even before birth. As early as the 1960's, tests indicated that babies go to sleep faster to the recorded sound of a human heartbeat or any similarly rhythmic sound. . . ." We found this to be true when little Matthew, Patti and Scott's son (now four), was born. Scott's father gave him a stuffed bear with a music box inside that produced the rhythmical beat like that of the mother's womb. He did sleep more restfully when he slept with that particular bear.

From the time of conception, our three children were exposed to the rhythm and sounds of music. TV was in its infancy, so we spent many hours around the piano, playing and singing. This was especially true with Cynthia, our firstborn. I would place her in her bassinet beside the piano as I practiced and push her throughout the house as I worked from one room to another. She slept with soft music coming from the radio when I wasn't at the piano. We sang to her constantly when we were feeding and dressing her; not only lullabies, but children's songs, as well as popular songs and hymns. As our family grew, this pattern was followed and music became a life-style.

Some might question, "Don't you ever give the child a chance to rest?" In answer: to this day all three of our children love to sleep with music playing softly in the background. Maybe music does "soothe the savage breast!"

There were and are multitudinous opportunities for exposure to all types of music: school symphony programs, church music presentations, library listening, musical productions on TV and in theaters, and numerous others. Children need to be introduced to all kinds of music and encouraged to form an appreciation for each.

We taught our children to find value and enjoyment in the ways music can give expression, from the foot-patting rhythm of country and gospel music to majestic hymns, to the arias of a grand opera, and the symphonic excellence of a well-performed classical piece.

We felt that our efforts were being rewarded when we often found all three of the children had turned away from a TV program to listen to a record. One memorable picture is their sitting on the floor around their small record players, listening to *Peter and the Wolf*. In that musical piece, their imaginations were stirred by the sounds of the instruments giving an exciting mental image of the animals in the story. Music can excite a child's imagination and be as captivating as "Pac Man" or any other video character.

As evidenced by how small children unconsciously learn the words and music to many TV commercials, they can be taught to sing the melodies of great music, as well as the little children's songs.

Recently we were in New London, Texas, for a revival, when a longtime friend of ours, Glennie Posey, came over from Henderson for a service. Posey had been in charge of the nursery at Broadway Baptist Temple Church in Houston when all three of our children were babies. Cynthia was about six months old when we joined the fellowship of that church, and immediately Posey became her "other" grandmother.

When Patti was born, nearly four years later, Posey was standing in our front door to greet us as we brought the new baby home. Tombo, born in California, was eighteen months old when we returned to Houston, where Brother Tom became associate pastor of the same church. We handed the baby to Posey.

As we sat around the table after lunch that day in New London, Posey reminded us, "Well, I still say I was with Cynthia when she made her first money singing." We laughed and asked when that was.

"Remember when Cynthia was two, Brother Tom was in the Marine Corps, you went to work, and I kept Cynthia for you? One day I took her to town to shop. It was Christmastime, and carols were being played almost on every corner. As we walked down the street, Cynthia was singing along at the top of her voice.

"When we started to go into a shop, she tugged at my hand, and said, 'Posey, hold my monies,' and she opened her tight little ball of a fist and dropped several coins into my hand.

" 'Where did you get this?' I asked her.

" 'The mens gib it to me,' she replied, as if it was ordinary for a little girl to receive money for her singing. As we had been walking along the street, men would slip a nickel or two into her hands."

We were blessed because our churches gave opportunities for children to sing. As I have mentioned, each of the children soloed somewhat at the age of three years. Cynthia's debut came after listening faithfully to a *Golden Record* about Samuel. She performed it word for word, inflections and all, in a children's program in front of the whole church.

Three-year-old Patti whistled her way into "fame" in that church at King City, California and continued singing with Cynthia or groups of cherub-like singers until she sang her first "real" solo at the age of eight in a Christmas program at the First Baptist Church of Jewett, Texas, when she sang, "That First Christmas."

Tombo, after that try at three when he couldn't seem to emit a note, sang with his sisters in trios and in the children's choirs and special groups at school. His first major solo came when he was twelve, and he carried the tenor solo part of the cantata, "Love Transcending" with the choir at our church, Hot Wells Baptist in San Antonio. Like the girls, after that first solo, he began to sing whenever he was asked.

During our college days, when Cynthia was about five, we discovered a song that seemed made for her, "I Don't Have to Wait . . . until I'm grown up." The last line says, "To be what Jesus wants me to be."

One of our firm convictions is that singers, especially children, should sing within the realm of their experiences. In other words, it sounds strange for a small child to sing:

> I was sinking *deep* in sin,
> Far from the peaceful shore,
> Very *deeply stained* within, . . .[16]

Just for the record—we do believe in the total depravity of every person, but a small child has not lived enough to have some of the experiences that are spoken of in some songs.

Having become a Christian about this time, Cynthia understood the words of verse three to the song

> If I'm old enough to love my parents,
> I can know Jesus' love;
> I can learn to trust Him and obey Him,
> For He watches above.
> —Harold Deal and Harry Dixon

She communicated her understanding of what she was singing, and many hearts have been blessed and challenged by a child's rendition of this simple song.

It is often difficult to find songs within a child's realm of experience, but there are many beautiful ones, such as "I Am a Promise" and "He's Still Working on Me." Many of the stirring hymns of faith that magnify the Father can be sung by children.

Not only are we to select the best songs for a child to sing but very gently and wisely, we must lead them to know that there is a time and place to share their song, and they are to blend their voices with others to bring forth the best performance of all.

This calls to mind a little girl's sitting in a principal's office, there to be punished because she became overzealous.

While we attended the University of Corpus Christi, Cynthia and I could go to school together. While she was in kindergarten, I was doing my practice teaching. One day the bell rang, it was time for recess, and my class rushed out the door. In spite of my admonishing them to take their time, each child wanted to take advantage of every second of the play period. All too soon, it was time to line up and begin their march back into the building. As we were passing the principal's office, we heard a child sobbing quietly. I stopped the marchers and looked into the office. There sat Cynthia, almost submerged in a big, overstuffed chair. Her head was bowed, almost touching her lap, and she was crying as if all hope were gone. I touched her gently and asked, "Honey, what is the matter?"

When she realized who it was, the tears really began to flow, and she tried to talk but couldn't make any sense. With a heartbreaking sob, she finally got out, "I—I—I—sang *too loud*!"

About this time, Miss Howard, the principal, came around the corner, but seeing me, stepped back to let me continue talking to Cynthia.

I put my arms around her and asked, "You sang too loud? Well, now, tell me all about it."

Later, controlling herself somewhat, she gulped out, "Miss Howard said I was singing too loud and made me come in here to wait." Miss Howard came in then and said sweetly, "Cynthia, let's tell Mother all about it," and turning to me, she explained, "I had the kindergarten group in the chapel for their singing lesson. Twice I had to call Cynthia down for singing louder than the other children. After the third time I just told her to come in here and sit until we were through."

Reaching out to Cynthia, she put her arms around her and said, "Now, Cynthia, come here and let me love you, and next time be sure you listen to me and don't sing louder than the other boys and girls. Will you please do that?"

Cynthia nodded her head, and we dried her tears. I left to take my children back to our room, and Cynthia stayed a few more minutes to visit with Miss Howard, who then took Cynthia back to her own class.

A scene to remember—just a little child—being punished in the principal's office and having to learn a big lesson that we must sing our songs together as one voice.

It is a delight to watch little ones sing together in a group, such as a "Booster Band" or "Crown Choir," as it was sometimes called when the children were little. Each little singer, singing with all his might, often forget the others around him, being so eager to sing his song. Opportunities such as these laid a rich foundation for songs and choruses that have become a part of their musical heritage. Even today, we enjoy singing from one chorus to another as we travel in the car together or at a family get-together. One chorus reminds us of another and so on.

Memories—images come back with music. Each song stands for a particular incident, and it takes us back in time to some happy occasion or perhaps some trying time when music led us through.

Patti recalls one of her earliest memories of a song when she was four.

Brother Tom was pastoring the Del Monte Baptist Church in Pacific Grove, California, and we made a trip to Fresno for a state Training Union convention. Since this was in the early years (1956) of Baptist work in California, our churches were small, and associational and state meetings were always anticipated because of much joy and fellowship.

That year we met in a hotel at Fresno, without any baby care provided, so we had to take our babies, Patti, four and Tombo, six months, with us to all the meetings. Patti recently recalled this and said, "I'll never forget—the soldiers marching in singing "Onward Christian Soldiers."

At first, I couldn't remember anything about "soldiers," but as we continued to talk and share the memories, we remembered that several men had dressed as soldiers and came marching in during the fellowship time, singing.

A musical image from a four-year-old's past.

We do not have to wait until a child is of school age or grown up to help them develop an ear for music. It must be a daily exercise. Patti recalls that even while cranking a gallon of ice cream her daddy (he was the ice cream maker at our house) would sing with them to keep the rhythm steady. She said, " 'Jesus Loves Me' always seemed to fit the best."

Sometimes it was good to have a planned activity each week. At our house in the early years of the children's musical training, we started what we called "Classics Night." It was not unusual for someone to yell from the living room, "Hey, did you forget it's classics night? Come on—no TV until we've listened to a record from the 'greats.' "

You would've thought such would be a boring time for the children, but instead they actually looked forward to it.

Once when Brother Tom was out visiting he stopped by a record shop and found an album called "Honky Tonk Classics: an Adventure in Stereophonic Sound" (we had just purchased our first stereo), as played by Mike Di Napoli on the piano. Everyone was crazy about it from the first time we played it, but I said, "If we're going to listen to this version, I think we should hear the 'real thing' also, don't you?" Thus began "Classics Night." Some of the family favorites were: Tschaikovsky's "Piano Concerto #1" ("Tonight We Love"), Chopin's "Polonaise in A Flat," "Lieberstraum," "Minuet in G," and others.

We had a spoof of the "Minuet in G" on a Spike Jones album, and the kids would try to imitate the sounds of the players. (Some may remember Spike Jones and his unusual band. They played the classics and pop songs with strange sound effects and hammed it up.) But when we put on an album played by a Philharmonic orchestra, the kids' mood would change. They drank in each note played.

Also, we would introduce some popular poetry such as the "Raggedy Man."

> The Raggedy Man,
> Oh, the Raggedy man,
> He works for paw
> And he's the funniest man
> You ever saw.
> —Author Unknown

This was Tombo's project when he was about four, and he had tremendous fun reciting it.

Since the children grew up in the parsonage, we had to guard our family time and make every minute count. Mealtimes could be rather hectic with the phone or the doorbell ringing. We tried to make our meals a fun experience, a relaxing time for sharing. But one of the "laws of the Medes and the Persians" around our house was, "Do not sing at the table."

Why, I don't really know, and it was a law we often found hard to keep because someone or something would always remind us of a song.

A song well remembered is "Can-ta-lou-pe, have some can-ta-lou-pe" sung to the tune of "Alouette."

This song was born one torrid summer day while we were on vacation. In the middle 1960s we found the ideal vacation spot for a family—a ranch at Mountain Home, Texas. It was a "dude" ranch without any "dudes," because it was run by a Christian couple who really guarded their clientele. If you were looking for the usual dude ranch with horses, hayrides, heated pool, and organized activities, this was not the place for you.

We swam in the North Fork of the Guadalupe River, which winds down a rocky creek bed and plays hide and seek along the way. It makes its appearance on the ranch in two places: the "Blue Hole," a deep, clear pond where the adult and older children could swim, and the cow tank where even the smallest child was safe paddling around in the water on rubber mats or surfboards.

Only one time have we seen the river on a rampage. After several days of hard rain, a flash flood made a frightening torrential sweep over the swimming holes and rushed madly to meet the bigger Guadalupe River.

Each summer for a week or two, all seven cabins on the ranch would be filled with our friends from Houston. The usual custom was for each family to provide breakfast and lunch in their own cabins, and supper was the "let's-put-it-together" type, in which everyone took part.

One day Tombo's friend was sharing lunch with us. When Brother Tom was helping the children's plates and passing the cantaloupe, he burst into song—"Can-ta-lou-pe! Have some can-ta-lou-pe" to the tune of "Alouette." We all joined in with our best operatic voices and motioned for our little guest to join us. He later told his mother, "I want to have lunch with the Clawsons again—they get to sing at the table." Really, the rule was broken more often than it was kept. I would not advise this being done in the best restaurants or at a formal dinner, but around the family table it makes for closeness that will long be remembered.

Those precious years of early childhood are gone far too soon. Plant songs like you would flowers in a garden and there will be perennial spring.

6

School Days

School Days, School Days,
Dear old golden rule days,
Reading and writing and 'rithmetic,
Taught by the tune of a hickory stick.
—W. D. Cobb and Gus Edwards

School days around the Clawson household were probably no different from hundreds of other homes where three children, a mama, and occasionally a daddy, were going to school each day. We went our separate ways each morning, living out our own experiences and gathering back home around 4:00 to share the happenings of the day.

For several years we had the privilege of being in the same schools, and I even taught Cynthia in the fourth grade. That was rather frustrating to her at first, because she was worried about what she should call me—"Mother" or "Mrs. Clawson." We decided that Mother was OK. The class became so used to it that once one of the girls asked me a question and she started, "Mother . . ." and then, with dismay, blurted out, "Oh, I called you *mother,*" as if to apologize.

Putting my arms around her I said, "That's all right. I'm probably with you more than your own mother, so I'll just be your daytime mother."

When we think of those "sharing times" after school, I am reminded of our seminary days in Fort Worth.

Because I had been unable to find a teaching position in Fort Worth that first year, the family was forced to be separated since the children and I lived in Duncanville, thirty-five miles away, where I taught English in the junior high school.

The first few weeks of the school year, Brother Tom tried to stay with us but found that he couldn't put in his library time and be on the road as much as necessary; so he lived in the dormitory during the week.

Each Friday afternoon, he would come for us. After we loaded our luggage in the back of the car, in went three children, the family dog Blackie, and three black kittens—David, Goliath, and Samanthie—who had been rescued from along the railroad tracks one black night. And we headed for Jewett. There we had our weekend home, the parsonage of the First Baptist Church. On Sunday nights we would make that same trek north to Duncanville, but with humans and animals tired and sleepy. Like most seminarians and their families, we stayed tired.

In the first few minutes of those drives on Fridays we would try to crowd in a whole week with all of us excitedly talking at once. Brother Tom was always loaded with the latest seminary jokes; one or more of us had learned a new song; Patti would relate the continuing saga of life in the fourth grade; and Cynthia and I would relate the happenings at the junior high.

On one memorable trip Brother Tom brought along a tape recorder for which he had traded a book that week. He hung the mike over the rearview mirror. At first we were all conscious of its hanging there, but after a few miles, we became so caught up in our sharing that we forgot about it. Later, when we played it back, we realized there had been *five* conversations going on at the same time. We had to make up for lost time.

I usually kept a book set aside especially for Fridays and would read to all after we settled down. During the week the children would ask me to reveal the next episode, but I would reply, "No, it's for the trip." During those years instruments other than the piano were being added to our household as the children were beginning their band classes. Cynthia began her band career in the fifth grade at Yoakum as she chose the B Flat clarinet for her instrument.

At Yoakum we were quickly initiated into country living. Growing up in Houston, we hardly knew what to expect. The parsonage and church stood on an acre of ground, cut from the corner of someone's corn field. None of us slept too well those first few weeks, as we listened to the night sounds that were magnified by the quietness of the country: the crickets, the cicadas, the faraway hooting of the owls, and the snorting of the cows as they shifted their weight while sleeping.

Brother Tom was paid a salary of forty-five dollars a week, plus all the eggs, milk, fresh garden vegetables, and meat we needed from the members—and lots of love. We accepted the church with the stipulation that I could teach. I was welcomed into the entire school system where I was *the* music teacher, second only to the band director, and held an honored position, supported by the faculty and the parents as well.

My responsibilities included the junior and senior high girls' choir and the two elementary schools—all grades. Both of our girls were in my classes.

The schools had gone several years without a music teacher. I met the high school girls' chorus each afternoon, the junior high girls' chorus three times a week, the fifth and sixth grades twice a week, and once a week fit in the other grades at the two elementary schools.

The junior high school met in the old building that had been the high school; I used the auditorium and a large room of the building for a music room. At first the piano was on the stage in the auditorium and was about as dilapidated as the building in which it rested.

Conditions and instruments are not always ideal, whether in schools or churches, banquet halls, or elsewhere. Especially in places where the piano hasn't been tuned in a long time, the instruments are usually so antiquated they are museum material. I have actually played the piano, at the same time trying to pry up the keys that have stuck.

The piano in the junior high building was a disaster. It really was beyond tuning, and after being assured that the school system didn't have the money for a new one, I of course did the best I could.

One day, I discovered the piano on a lower level in front of the stage. I did wonder about it, but thinking this would be better (I would be closer to my students) I didn't inquire why it wasn't on stage.

I sat down to play and was horrified at the sound that came out and the sound that did *not* come out. It was impossible to play. About that time, the janitor, who had been listening out in the hall, came in and said, "I'm sorry about the piano, Mrs. Clawson. We were sweeping the stage last night so's you could have a clean room. We moved the piano too close to the edge, and it fell off the stage. When we tried to pick it up, the outside came off."

"You mean that the insides came out of the case?" I managed to ask tremblingly in my horror.

"Yes, ma'am, but we got it back together. I hope it works."

I merely sat there for a minute or two and then limply said, "Thank you, I guess it'll be all right," knowing in my heart that it was beyond resurrection.

At lunch, I called Brother Tom and told him about the piano. He would be right down. (He's always so helpful and comes running to fix whatever is wrong.) Now, he didn't know much about tuning a piano; he could tune his guitar, but with his sturdy wrench and hammer in hand, he came to my rescue. Believe it or not, he did get it in tune enough that when I played a song it was recognizable. I hope when I get to heaven I'll always have new pianos to play on.

By then, Cynthia had started her lessons on the clarinet and practiced each day as soon as she came home from school.

One night, as I was finishing the supper dishes, I yelled from the kitchen, "She's calling the cows up!" Cynthia was on the back porch diligently practicing, beginner that she was. With the screeching sounds she was producing, she must have struck a beckoning call, because from out of the darkness came the mournful lowing of a cow.

In the weeks that followed, either she must have become more proficient on the clarinet or the cows must have become accustomed to the strange sound made by that black stick she held in her mouth.

While the future "Miss Benny Goodman" was producing cow-calling sounds on the back porch, first-grader Patti was at the piano in the living room practicing her scales up and down the keyboard. Tombo, age three, not wanting his big sisters to outshine him musically, was running through the house tooting on his toy trumpet.

The piano was always the pivot around which the children's musical expression was the most apparent, but each chose other instruments to help them enlarge their scope of music.

Take for example, Patti's accordion. While we lived in Jewett, Patti had become enthralled with this instrument while watching one of Cynthia's friends playing. For her tenth birthday she was given a twelve-base accordion. She began her study with our friend Alice. With her background on the piano Patti was able to develop a nice technique quickly.

The accordion has been a source of personal enjoyment for her, and also a means of service. At Christmas time, when the family would go caroling, she would accompany us. Since she has grown up, she continues to use the same twelve-base accordion in her ministry, such as at jail services, retreats, and socials. Last year she had a delightful time giving a program for the children's storytime at the public library in San Antonio. The children sat spellbound as she played and sang for them.

Recalling another time her instrument came in handy, she relates how she accompanied the church choir from Manor Baptist Church, as they floated down the San Antonio River on barges, caroling the Christmas strollers.

Like Cynthia, she chose the B Flat clarinet for her band instrument, but she didn't get to call up the cows since we lived in the city by then. Cynthia continued with the clarinet through junior and senior high schools in Duncanville and Houston.

One rewarding aspect of having children can come when we are able to walk with them the same academic hallways we had experienced. Being in the ministry and moving from here to there, we were surprised in 1963 to find ourselves back in Houston where Brother Tom and I had grown up.

Thinking far into the future as we bought a home shortly after we married, we looked for a house in walking distance of the three schools our children would someday attend. Of the three, Cynthia was the only child to attend one of those schools.

With a thrill I escorted Cynthia to the school in the hope of introducing her to some of my teachers, if they were still there.

I was shocked as we entered the band hall: the same director, Eugene Seastrand, greeted us at the door. And I thought, "Why, he's not old at all!" I remembered my high school days when, we all thought he must be at least a hundred years old! But now he didn't look any older than I. He must have been in his twenties then, because I recalled he had left school for the service in World War II. So he was only a few years older than I.

My brother had followed me in high school and was in the band. It was a standing joke in my family that I could hardly be expected to carry a piano in the marching band, so I had to be in the school orchestra, while my brother played the trumpet in the band.

Cynthia has fond memories of the three years she worked under Mr. Seastrand. In recent years, when he attended one of her concerts, she was overjoyed to see him.

Now I must mention another shock (call it a "cultural shock," if you will) I received, the first football game we attended with Cynthia playing in the band. It had been at least twenty years since I had been to a football game. To me the game was a three-ring circus! Of course, our main purpose for attending the game was to see Cynthia perform in the band, but we also wanted the football boys to win for the honor of our school.

We couldn't watch every move on the field because of all the activities going on right in front of the stands. During the game, the band not only played but carried on all kinds of stunts and skits before us.

At one point, the officers of the band walked over to the other band and presented themselves to the officers of that band; then they would bring back the other officers to be introduced to our band. Just before halftime, the band had to assemble on the side of the field, line up in position, and mark off their steps while standing in front of us. Then, they marched to the end of the field back of the goalpost, ready to march onto the field as soon as the whistle blew—all of this going on while the poor football players were struggling with all their might to carry the ball across the goal line.

What capped it off for me came later in the game when our boys were down on the five-yard line, fighting with every muscle to hold the line—and the entire pep squad, some 150 girls, filed out—it was time for their break! I really don't remember if our boys won that night, and no one else seemed to care!

As we look back on those hectic days around our house, we wouldn't take anything for them. American homes today can often become like that football game—a three-ring circus—especially if there are several children in the family all trying to go in different directions. Schedules must be juggled, plans often changed at the last minute when someone comes from home to announce, "I forgot to tell you, but I've got to be back at school by 6:30. We're having a special called meeting for that concert Friday night. Sorry!" "Miss Junior High" calls out from her room, "But, I have to be at *my* piano lesson at 6:30, and you know I can't drive," and it's visitation night at the church. What to do? Well, somehow the musicians always arrived at their appointed times, and Mama and Papa would fall into bed at night, exhausted.

We wanted the children to be part of all the musical opportunities the school curriculum could afford. We found that the majority of the band members were among the finest students academically and socially, from homes where parents did care and seemed to be more actively involved with their children.

Have you ever lived in a house with a set of drums? We have, and that is an experience all to itself. We could never escape the rat-a-tat-tat of the snare drum, the clang of the cymbals, or the thump, thump of the bass drum being stomped by a size 11 shoe. Tombo was our drummer, and we knew that someday, somehow, he would make "music" out of that noise coming from his room.

He began his band stint at Houston in the fourth grade, and for three years played the trumpet. When he entered junior high in San Antonio, he looked longingly at the percussion section and decided that was for him. While he was taking lessons on the drum, he continued playing the cornet, to which his director had changed him that first day. Before the year was out, he was in the drum section.

For Christmas that year, we gave him a trap set. When we opened our gifts on Christmas Eve, we found under the tree a gift that had been put there without our knowledge. On the card was written, "For the family that has everything—including a set of drums," signed John Roark. John, one of the deacons in the church, was an instructor on the rifle range at Lackland Air Force Base. We laughed when we opened the gift to find a pair of shooter's earmuffs! The next Sunday, when we thanked him for them, I said, "That's a nice gift, John, but you should have given us five pairs. Everyone is fighting over that one pair."

By the time Tombo was in the ninth grade, he auditioned for and won a place as second chair drummer in the All-City Junior High Band. He never got to perform with that band because the week before the spring concert, he was in a car accident. As a result he lost the last six weeks of his final year in junior high.

In the fall, he was accepted in the "A" band at high school, but due to the head injury, he couldn't wear the hat to the band uniform and was not able to march with the band during football season.

At each football game, they would use Tombo in some halftime stunt.

Once, he was a tall Mickey Mouse which the girls escorted onto the field,
and they went through their planned routine. He always had fun clown-
ing around, but he was anxious to be a genuine part of the band. At
concert time around Christmas, he stood tall and straight in the percussion section and finally felt at home.

Tombo recalls the first time that he did march with the band—the first
game of his junior year: "Music has always been the mainstay in my life.
Now, as far as *what* makes the music—that is the thing. The first maker
of music, that set down the basics, was the church. Since we were raised
in a preacher's home, you might usually expect that church music was
the most we heard. But being from a musical family, too, I was shown
the other music makers I would come to know.

"I started singing like everybody else does, I guess: singing in choirs
at church and school; singing alto in a choir in the fourth grade; or even
a boy's choir in the sixth grade. But as you get a little older, your voice
begins to do strange things when you least expect it. So, for a while I tried
out the band.

"One of the all-time greats in high school is halftime at the football
games. It was my first. On top of that, it was the first out-of-town game
for the year, up in Austin.

"The weather was pretty hot and humid, which made us perspire just
sitting in the stands, much less marching.

"On top of our heads—remember the point to the story—was a rather
tall hat we wore with our uniforms. A la Fred Flintstone—Buffalo
Lodge. Anyway, inside that hat was a string you would tie so the hat
would fit your head and stay in place. Well, being the first time to march,
freshman that I was, I didn't know you were supposed to tie the string
since that hat seemed to have a good fit around my head.

"Little did I know that as we began to march and sweat that soon my
hat (Buffalo Lodge, remember?) was beginning to drop completely
around my head. I was the bass drum player for the band, and between
alternating beats of the drum with drumsticks in my hand, with one I
would beat the drum and with one I would attempt to push my hat up,
at least above my eyes so I could see where I was going. That was the
longest halftime!

"The next week, my dad's secretary who had been at the game, asked
him what I was doing. She thought it was perhaps a ritual the freshmen

went through—to beat the drum with one stick and to beat your head with the other. Boom! Boom! Boom!"

Music and the band helped to ease the frustration and disappointment fifteen-year-old Patti had felt when we moved from Houston to San Antonio during the summer before she entered senior high school. I remember her complaining, "I'll go to San Antonio, but I'll hate it!" That lasted about two weeks. Patti was especially disturbed because she had to leave her boyfriend and her other friends.

The folks at Hot Wells welcomed us with open arms, and in a few weeks Patti captured the heart of the most eligible young man in the youth department. Of course, this didn't make her so popular with some of the girls, but it wasn't long before they were all sharing good times together.

In the band, she immediately found a school family; everyone had a common interest—music. It was football season and marching time, so she didn't have time to feel "new and alone."

Again we were surprised to find that her director was also an old friend of ours—Ken Turner. We had gone to college with him and his wife Ginger when Patti was just a baby. In recent years, Patti has worked with him once again in a different capacity, since she was church pianist at her church, and the Turners came to serve as interim music director and organist. Patti counts that as one of the rich blessings in her life.

Parades for special holidays, fiestas, and livestock shows were fun for the band—but hard work, too.

Cynthia's first parade, at the tender age of eight, came when she marched in the Butterfly Parade at Pacific Grove, California. That parade marks the beginning of a week's activities to welcome the Monarch butterflies, which migrate to the same trees in Pacific Grove each fall.

Her only disappointment was that she didn't get to dress like a butterfly as most of the children did. For open house at her school that week, she had a special part in a musical number and sang the solo of a little shepherd girl, so she had to wear her costume and tend her sheep along the parade route. Two songs from that program were: "Que Sera, Sera" and "Poor Little Robin."

San Antonio is a city of many parades. The bands were not to perform in the rain, but in Texas a sprinkle is just humidity. The kids often came home with woolen band uniforms hanging limply, mud splattered, and tattletale signs of marching behind the trail riders. It is usually raining or ice-cold as the parades wend their way among the tall buildings, cold wind slapping them in the face as they round a corner. In Cynthia's first stock show parade in Houston, she wore her granddaddy's "long handles" because of the freezing weather.

Patti recalls one parade that seemed interminable since she had been ill the days preceding it. She jokingly admits: the only reason she survived the seven-mile trek was the handsome blond French hornplayer she was enamored with was directly in front of her, and her favorite trombonist was behind her, giving an encouraging boost with his slide.

Tombo always had an extra load, the bass drum, to support, and a parade is the time a drummer can cut loose with as much power as his drum can muster.

Our first year in San Antonio, Patti found another involvement which proved to be a challenge. She sang in the Campus Life Singers, a select ensemble chosen from the San Antonio high schools. The group performed for school, churches, and civic organizations. Through it she was able to meet many young Christians from churches and schools in the area where they were invited to sing.

The piano remained Patti's first love, and she worked hard at developing her skills and technique. Although she learned many classical solos well, she seemed to gravitate naturally towards accompanying. Patti recently noted, "While I was studying with other teachers, Mother and Daddy both tried to instill within me the art of accompanying singers and instrumentalists." In high school, she was used as accompanist for solo and ensemble contests, youth choirs, and young performers. Along with the piano, she began playing the organ and filled in when our church organist was absent.

Years later, when Patti was nineteen, she was called as the organist at Morgan Avenue Baptist Church in Corpus Christi. When the church called to see if she would be interested, she answered, "Yes, but I'll have to pray about it." We reminded her that churches usually can't pay a living wage for their organists, and since she didn't have a job, she should be aware of that before talking with the church.

After spending a weekend with the church, she reported that she had accepted. We asked, "What about the salary?"

She looked rather funny and answered, "They'll give me fifteen dollars a Sunday, but," she quickly assured us, "I prayed about it! And it's what the Lord wants me to do." We all laughed and said in unison, "Romans 8:28!" She then explained that she had already accepted a job at Sears, so she could make a living.

Life is often like a ladder, as we add year upon year, but so is it like a cycle—we seem to circle back to the beginning again. Morgan Avenue was the church where Brother Tom was baptized at age thirteen. It was called Central Baptist Church then, and was an old tabernacle-type building down on the waterfront. The name was changed when the new building was built on top of the seawall. So Patti was to be a member there. We are constantly astonished at the direction of our paths.

I recall another time when we were made aware of life's cycle.

It was 1973 and Tombo was a member of the San Antonio Youth Chorale, a group of young musicians chosen from the high schools in the city, and they were to perform as a part of the week's celebration of "Joske's Special Days."

Different schools, organizations, musical groups, dance teams, and art groups had been invited to perform throughout the store. On the first floor, one might see a group of fiddlers, while across the aisle and down in another department you could see a group of Spanish dancers doing the hat dance. On the next floor, a glass blower would be set up or an artist painting a portrait while his customer modeled before him. Clowns glided among the crowd in the store and played little games with the children.

We went to the fifth floor furniture department where the chorale group would sing. Looking around for a place to sit, we noticed that others were sitting on the beds, low stools, or anywhere they could. We sat down on the nearest bed to the aisle, right in front of the risers where the choir would stand.

In a few minutes, the young people filed in, lined up, and began to sing.

As we listened, I turned to Brother Tom and asked, "Does this place remind you of something?"

Taking my hand, he smiled and replied, "Sure, our honeymoon."

We had spent our honeymoon in San Antonio, twenty-seven years before. Because it had been our first time to visit San Antonio (and we had always heard of Joske's of Texas, as it was called in those days), we had spent one whole morning exploring all the floors and departments. Of course, we didn't purchase anything, for we had little money. But we spent many hours "oohing," "aahing," and wishing.

That day, as Tom and I listened to that fine group of young people and smiled at our son, we could hardly believe the years had passed so quickly. So long ago we couldn't possibly have pictured this day and how a son of ours would be sharing his gift of music.

While all three of the children did enjoy their band experiences—the football games, the parades, the trips, and the concerts—the piano was for Patti a number-one means of expressing her song, while singing ran a close second. Singing really was numero uno for Tombo and Cynthia.

Both took part in the choral groups of their schools, and each won a place in the All-State High School Choir. In her senior year, Cynthia won from Houston and went to Dallas for the concert. Eight years later, Tombo was one of two young men from the San Antonio district to win. For both occasions the rest of the family found their place in the audience, giving support by our presence.

A highlight for the children during their school years was the privilege to sing in a thousand-voice choir for the 1966 Billy Graham Crusade in the Astrodome at Houston. Tombo, being only ten, really prided himself in being able to do that. The theme song, "Heaven Came Down," became everyone's favorite from the first rehearsal.

The children sang it going to the Astrodome, at the Astrodome, and on the way home from the Astrodome. In fact, that was the only song they sang for weeks.

As an extracurricular activity in high school, Cynthia formed a Peter, Paul, and Mary-type trio with two of her friends, Dwight Morris and Brian Martin, and they performed at banquets, "hootenannies," church, and school activities. We can still hear, "You Take a Stick of Bamboo, You Take a Stick of Bamboo," "Puff, the Magic Dragon," and other pop songs of the 1960s. They were in demand, and many times had to choose between performing every night or doing their schoolwork. Lessons had to win sometimes.

She was chosen to take part in an all-city talent review, the "Kaleidoscope," from the Houston high schools, which was held at the University of Houston. This was the first really big performance she had been involved in, other than singing in the *Messiah* with the Union Baptist Association at Christmastime. The night of the talent review, she poured out her heart and soul when she stood and sang "More," not so much for the honor she might gain, but for that special boy who was sitting in the audience. We didn't think he had ever caught on that it was meant just for him—one of those one-sided high school crushes.

Cynthia sang at every opportunity in schools, churches, civic programs, luncheons, or banquets. Many times young vocal hopefuls will ask her how one gets started singing. She advises them to be willing to sing anytime they are asked—even to sing for their supper, if nothing else. There were always talent shows at school, camps, church youth activities—anything to give practice for performing before people.

Talent shows at school can sometimes be the highlight of the year, as you watch the young people begin to spread their wings—some seemingly with very little talent but loads of courage; those who have never been able to share their talent before; and some who have marvelous promise.

One talent show that stands our was during the year Patti was a senior. She sang "Kansas City . . . here I come" in the inimitable style of Sophie Tucker.

When she first sang this piece at home, we were aghast that this voice was coming from our "sweet" little girl. It was another side of Patti we hadn't learned.

Without her knowledge, Cynthia and three of her friends from Howard Payne University had driven to San Antonio, arriving just as the program began to give Patti their support. I think Patti sang a little better knowing she had a rooting section in the audience. Big Sister had given her a little advice backstage before the time came. "Patti, start belting it out before the curtain rises completely. Grab the audience." And that she did.

Tombo's talent lay not only in singing, but also in acting. In his senior year he played a red-haired "Li'l Abner." This was his first big stage production, but he came across like a trouper.

Like Cynthia and Patti, he sang anytime he could, merely for the joy of singing. From elementary school on, he performed many times in school musical programs. He recalled singing with a group of sixth grade boys, dressed as cowpokes and doing "The Streets of Laredo" for a PTA meeting.

In the sixth grade he was given a place in the San Antonio Boys' Choir, a special group of boys from all over the city. This was good training for him.

In the spring of 1968, "Hemisfair" was opened in San Antonio, and all three had opportunity to take part in the activities at different times.

One Saturday the Boys' Choir, with each little boy dressed as a cowboy, stood on the steps of the Confluence Theater and gave a concert. The big event of the hour was the appearance of President Johnson, and the boys sang lustily. But I think that each boy was not so taken with the thought of seeing or even singing for the President, as they were in thinking about the time afterwards when with their *free* pass they were going to have the rest of the afternoon to try out all the rides, foods, and fun.

While Patti and Tombo were in junior and senior high school, I was teaching at the neighboring elementary school, Inez Foster, that "fed" into these schools; so many of their friends were my former students. I taught language arts and music for the nine years we were in San Antonio.

On Fridays we had Talent Day in our music classes. These were fourth and fifth graders who at first would protest, "I can't do anything—I can't sing like you do, Mrs. Clawson, and I can't play the piano, either."

So we would have a lesson on what constitutes talent. Everyone can do something better than someone else, however simple or grand it might be. I would ask such questions as: "Who can bake a cake?—that's a talent; who can read or write a poem?—that's a talent; who can work on a car? That's a talent," and then I would assure the boys that working on a car was certainly not my talent, and the like. Then my students began to do some thinking about what they *could* do.

I requested that on Thursday they tell me what they were going to do the next day, so I could decide if it could be done and how we would present it to the class. If it were twirling the baton and the weather permitted, I would lead the class outside and watch the performers. Some did gymnastics. How often this opened up the timid soul or became an encouragement to the slow learner.

I remember one fifth grader who had been a headache to all the teachers as he had come up through each grade. He was frustrated within himself and seemingly had few friends because he could not function socially.

When I had explained that cooking could be someone's talent, he had listened. That night at home he had his mother help him make enough candy out of gelatin for the entire class.

He came early to my class the following morning to tell me his mother would bring something to school by the 11 o'clock period when he would be in my music class. Between each class that morning, he would appear at my door to ask if his mother had arrived. Eleven o'clock came, classes changed, and he ran into the room, inquiring once more, "Did she come?"

I hated to tell him no, but she hadn't. His face fell and he quietly sat down, all interest in the class gone. Fifteen minutes had gone by, and several had already performed, when there was a knock at the door. He was up and at the door before I could make it. He had seen his mother coming as he was looking out the window. She apologized for being late, but this didn't matter to him, since she was finally there. With eyes sparking and pride written all over his face, he accepted the aluminum-foil-covered plate from his mother's hands. Handing it to me, he declared proudly, "I made these."

I turned to the class and explained that we would now have our refreshments and share in his talent. He would be our host. I reached for the napkins and followed him around the room, placing a napkin on each student's desk. Then he would place a piece of candy in the middle. He walked mannerly around the room, smiling like a Cheshire cat, and when he had finished, he sat down, not eating, with such great pride as he watched us devouring his "talent."

After all, what is a talent for, but to share with your friends? A talent or gift—call it what you may—is given only to be given away.

About this time, I tried adding the guitar to my means of making music. The guitar was a household staple around our house, but I had never really thought about trying to play it—that was Brother Tom's instrument—but now, each of the kids was practicing and becoming adequate guitarists. Brother Tom laughs about his "seven chords" but he enjoys the few songs he can play. Tombo became more proficient than anyone else in the family and used the guitar quite often in church, youth meetings, banquets, and such.

The music department of the school district decided to provide guitar lessons for any of the teachers who were interested. So once a week, several of the teachers from my school would drive across town after school. In a class of about fifty teachers, we would strum out "Country Roads" and "Paper Roses." It was a riot! Strum, strum—count, count— bend those fingers around that neck and try to sing at the same time, "Paper roses, paper roses . . ." About the time I began to put my chords together and make "music," I fell at school and broke my right arm! That was the end of my guitar playing.

My fellow guitarists continued in the class, and at the last PTA meeting of the year, I accompanied them on the piano as they played and sang "Country Roads."

In life, school days can go on forever, for we never cease to learn, but there comes an end to our formal education and schoolhouse learning. For some it is their high school years while others go on to further training for the place they will take in society.

For all three of our children, college was a continuation of their musical interests since they were music majors and were involved in all the campus musical activities. Cynthia and Patti attended Howard Payne University at separate times. Tombo first went to Stephen F. Austin University for a semester and then returned home to work.

Churches began calling him for supply, and in the next two years he was music and youth director for two churches in San Antonio. In 1975 he accepted a position in the First Baptist Church of Nixon, a town about seventy miles south of San Antonio, where he would go on Sundays and Wednesday nights.

In the fall of 1977, wanting to continue his college education, he came to live with us in Conroe and enrolled in Sam Houston State University for a period. While here, he was music and youth director at New Waverly, a town near Huntsville, where he was in school.

School days in college comprise another story for each one—a bridge between childhood and the adult they would become. As a family, we shared these years as much as distance, telephone, and letters would permit. We made numerous trips to attend activities in which they participated.

School days are treasured days both by students and parents alike, and most families have albums full of memories soon packed away.

(Top) Tom and I, Virginia Wilbanks, started the family symphony on November 16, 1946. (Bottom) How time flies! In ten years the symphony was progressing. Patti (left), Tommy, Jr. (in lap), and Cynthia had joined in.

(Top) Patti, 3, and Cynthia, 6, all dressed up in their Sunday-go-to-meeting clothes (Bottom) "Tombo" looks awfully forlorn as his mother and sisters gathered 'round the piano (Christmas of 1958).

(Top Left) Tombo began his horn practice at the age of 3. (Top Right) Cynthia with her piano lessons, age 8 (Bottom Left) Cynthia with her first accordian (Bottom right) Fanny the pup was in the limelight with Patti and Tombo.

(Top Left) Patti and Cynthia "all gussied up" at Houston in 1964 (Top Right) By now you can spot all of us—Cynthia, Brother Tom, and I on the back; Tombo and Patti on the front, 1961. (Bottom) The family portrait at Hot Wells Baptist Church, San Antonio (1967)

(Top Left) Patti (left) and Cynthia in 1968—it's no wonder your eyes hurt! (Top Right) Brotherly and sisterly love—Cynthia and Tombo in 1968—Cynthia was a soph in college, Tombo a sixth grader. (Bottom) Tombo practicing at home.

(Top Left) Cynthia Clawson and Ragan Courtney after their wedding (Top Right) Debby and Tommy (Tombo) with little Nicholas (Bottom) Patti and Scott Berry after tying the knot

(Top) Cynthia and Lily Katherine have many happy times. (Bottom) How many grandmothers have a chance to introduce all their grandkids at one time? Will, Nicholas, and Matthew are in back with Lily and Andrew in front.

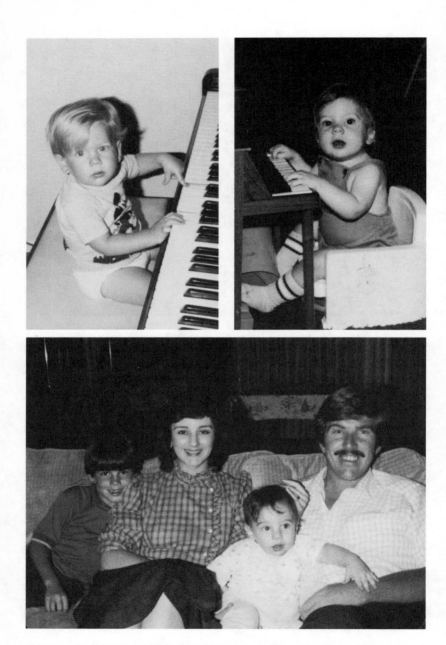

(Top Left) Will Courtney developing his keyboard manner (Top Right) Matthew Berry rehearsing for his first concert (Bottom) Debby and Tommy with Nicholas and baby Andrew

(Top) Patti sings and Cynthia plays as the rest of the family symphony listens. (Bottom Left) Does music ever run in the family! Andrew and Nicholas "tickle the ivories." (Bottom Right) Scott, Patti, and Matthew ready to "punch them cattle"

(Top) You didn't think I was gonna get by without pictures of great grandmas, did you? (left to right) Will, Brother Tom, Cynthia, "Ga Ga" (Brother Tom's mother Edna), and me. (Bottom) That's "Mamaw" (my mother Willie) with Cynthia, Lily, and me. And the beat goes on!

7
Sisters, Sisters

The ambulance came to a slow stop in front of the small, white-frame house. Jumping out and running to the back of the vehicle, the young father proudly helped the attendant with the mother and two little girls. He took the baby from the crib, placed her in the mother's arms, and lifting down the four-year-old, put her blanket-wrapped dolly in her arms, and headed her toward the house.

He turned back to guide the stretcher gently as it was being rolled into the house, bearing its precious cargo, the mother and her tiny, newborn baby.

Thus was the homecoming of the new little sister in the Clawson household, Patti Jean.

We had planned it all so well. There was to be a new baby in the house, but Cynthia, age four, was never to feel left out or unloved while so much attention would be given the new baby. Somewhere I read about a splendid idea, and we had decided to try it.

So there would be no jealousy of the family newcomer, we bought a baby doll and layette and presented it to Cynthia at the hospital on the morning of the day we were to carry the new baby home.

She proudly carried her baby down the hall, as I was being pushed by the ambulance attendant, followed by the nurse carrying baby Patti. It was quite a procession. Outside, her daddy put her in the back of the ambulance so she could ride with me and the new baby—and carry her new baby home, too.

Two little sisters—yet so different. Often they were dressed alike when they were small, and while the outward appearance might be similar,

103

they were true opposites on the inside. Their basic personalities are still unlike.

There were the normal sibling rivalries, but these never became paramount, never overshadowed their love and appreciation for one another, nor were they a truly disturbing element to family unity. Each problem was dealt with as quickly and quietly as possible.

Ours was not always a quiet home—noisy, yes—but most of the time there were happy sounds. Music constantly going on in some part of the house; children laughing and playing, and yes, fighting sometimes; Daddy yelling, "Let's quiet down!" when the noise level began to rise too much.

If their daddy was gone, and they thought I might be outside (next door perhaps), they would have a singing, "yelling" contest while washing dishes. One would sing a note—the other would try to top her—so the game could go on and on and on until they could finish their chores—anything to make chores more tolerable.

Of course, should they hear the car drive into the driveway and the door slam, their contest would turn into a lovely duet, usually a favorite "church" song that was their daddy's favorite. He would go over, put his arms across their shoulders, and begin harmonizing with them.

From the first day Patti was initiated into the Clawson Clan, the unique relationship of the girls was that "they had each other." Almost four years later, when Baby Tombo made his appearance, they may have thought, *now we have a real live toy to play with.* Tom and I thought we'd have to watch them so they wouldn't gang up on him, but it wasn't long before he made it quite apparent that he could handle the sisters.

When he was about four, he began begging for a brother. He would say, "The girls have each other, and I don't have anybody!" And we'd all quickly assure him that he was special—he was their *only* brother.

When the girls were small, no one would have mistaken one for the other—Cynthia with her dark red hair and Patti, pure blonde. It was a shock when Patti was eighteen, and someone thought she was Cynthia. For a long time, we couldn't see the close similarity, but it has become more apparent as they matured into adulthood.

As they reached their late teens, they began to share more in common adventures, as well as in clothes and hairstyles, often to the consternation of their friends who, when meeting them apart, would often mistake them for each other.

Since each of the children were four years apart in school years, only twice did Cynthia and Patti attend the same school—in their early elementary grades. Because of this, Patti often followed in Cynthia's footsteps. Much to her frustration she was often accused of trying to imitate Cynthia. Both of the girls attended Howard Payne University, Cynthia graduating in the spring of 1970 and Patti arriving in the fall, and this tended to be a problem. We had never thought of our family closeness as a problem, but it manifested itself in the girls having mannerisms in common.

Cynthia introduced Irving Berlin's song "Sisters."[17] into their musical repertoire, a true picture in words, when in her senior year at Howard Payne she starred in a musical variety concert called "Happy Daze."

The song was not listed in the printed program since Cynthia had planned a surprise for Patti. At home, they had been singing "Sisters" together for some time as they had sung through my old sheet music.

As usual, when Cynthia was in a special program and our schedule permitted, the four of us would drive to Brownwood to see the production.

That night Cynthia introduced her family and then asked Patti to come up onto the stage. As she walked up the aisle, the orchestra began playing that number, and Cynthia began singing to Patti. Most people thought the piece had been planned and well-rehearsed.

Cynthia had another surprise waiting for her daddy. After several more songs were sung, while the orchestra began the strain of "Daddy . . . My heart belongs to Daddy," she came out into the audience and, sitting in her daddy's lap, began to sing to him. If you know Brother Tom, you realize he had to reach for his handkerchief.

In 1972 Patti began traveling with Cynthia on the concert tours as her accompanist. The warm and humorous happenings along that trail would fill several books. Every year or so the girls have vowed to write a book—maybe someday, but in this chapter they want to share a few of the more memorable experiences.

Patti

"A ministering angel my sister shall be."—Shakespeare

Since Cynthia was the oldest, her responsibility often was to watch out for us. You can imagine how that generally sat with me—the middle child, next in line to the throne, the rebellious and independent one. No sister of mine, who was a mere three years and nine months older than I, was going to lord it over me with threats of "I'll tell Mother and Daddy!" So, it wasn't until Cynthia went to college and I was in high school that I saw the positive side of her watching out for me.

We were now sharing clothes (commonly called "hand-me-downs"), sharing evenings (still with a bit of a "little-sister's-in-the-back-seat attitude), sharing makeup (Cynthia will never let me forget about Daddy throwing away *her* green eyeshadow when I was caught wearing it to school), and, of course, sharing music. There were hundreds of hours spent sharing the piano bench when Cynthia would come home from college on the weekends and teach me all the latest songs. The "latest songs" could be anything from "People" to "Love Me with All of Your Heart" to a new arrangement of "Ragtime Cowboy Joe."

We had been taught an appreciation for all styles of music—classical to country—so it wasn't unusual that in college Cynthia was involved in classical lessons, a cappella choir, pop ensembles, and variety shows.

By the time I was ready to enter college (and since I already knew all the songs), I naturally followed her at Howard Payne University. It was there that our similarities provoked a variety of responses; and, although I admitted to having the same mannerisms, knowing the same songs, keeping the same friends, and wearing some of the same clothes, I definitely was "me." So I proved it by dropping out of school after a painful seven months. Christina Georgina Rossetti wrote:

"For there is no friend like a sister/In calm or stormy weather."

And so it went. Cynthia has many times rescued me from storms in my life. Through the years of traveling together, we developed an uncanny ESP between us, and it has proven to be lifesaving two or three times.

The interminably long seven months at college were devastating to me emotionally, and by the time I left, I had added several addictions to my life that will stay with me forever. I rode the waves from ebb tide to the highest, and it was during a period of chemically-induced highs (this time attributed to diet pills that I was given from a certain doctor in the "diet business") that Cynthia called and asked me to go on the road with her.

For six years I was her full-time accompanist, although I lived in a different town than she did during several periods. Often Cynthia would call and insist, "You need to be back on the road with me," and she could read me well.

Her acceptance of me, her belief in my artistic ability, and her hope for me in the future has been more than an anchor. She has given me the freedom to grow in different directions, but she gave me the stabilizing environment of Christian friends, many of whom were musicians, who could love me back to health.

One of our earliest medleys of songs included "Jesus Walked This Lonesome Valley." Many times when I played it during a performance, watching Cynthia sing, I wondered about Jesus' brothers and sisters. I've never walked a valley alone. Cynthia has always been there.

> "My sister! my sweet sister! if a name
> Dearer and purer were, it should be thine." —Byron

In the first year of traveling together, I learned that a hidden reward I received from our concerts was that Cynthia and I usually shared the same spiritual blessing. Many were the nights we talked for hours after a concert about the audience response, new insights on a song in the concert, or the blessings of new Christian friends we had met that day. We sentimentally reminisce about that first year when we were both still single.

Although we often had months where we did twenty or more concerts, our lives and goals seemed more simple. We still encountered cross-country plane trips with enthusiasm, whereas now we feel like one of a herd of cattle being shipped to another state. Every new hotel bed was met with energetic challenge to see who could jump the highest, whereas now we fall prostrate before the Lord and seek divine energy to make it through the evening.

After Cynthia and Ragan were first married, I asked him if she had clued him in to the fact our secret way of relieving anxiety and tension was to jump on the hotel beds. I'm sure the people on the floor below us loved it! It was a holdover from our childhood, but it wasn't until many years later that our folks discovered the reason for the unexplained, broken bed slats.

Sisterhood Is Powerful. —Robin Morgan

Although I hate to admit it, Cynthia was always a great barometer when it came to the male companions I kept. The adamant disagreements we've had in the past fourteen years have been few and far between, but I would dare say 50 percent of them have been over the issue of my male friends. Call it predestination or resignation, the Lord's will was ultimately done in my life, and when Scott and I married, Cynthia gladly gave her approval and sang a song that she and I had written for Scott.

I never had any doubts that I would love Ragan, but I was surprised at the instant affinity we had for each other. Perhaps it was because he understood my personal search for peace as he had traveled some of the same roads. Or perhaps it was because we both loved Cynthia so dearly. I felt an indescribable pride when Ragan introduced me at a concert and jokingly explained, "If I were a Mormon, Patti would be my second wife!"

No matter how close Cynthia and I are, there have been times that I hesitated to share a secret with her because she's still enough of an older sister to occasionally be a mother to me. Ragan has been the sounding board against which I bounced a lot of my questions and ideas. As we've all grown older, the late-night talks have been exchanged for lingering breakfast hours where we've drunk a second and third pot of coffee, exchanged lofty thoughts, and made profound theological discoveries!

Of course, those lazy mornings are few now that I'm not traveling with Cynthia and we are living several states apart. Last year, after not seeing us for several weeks, Cynthia and Ragan told Scott and me that they had sat dejectedly at their breakfast table in Nashville and longed to be drinking coffee with us in San Antonio. They had not known we were wishing the same thing.

Being on the road together produced an intimacy much like a marriage. Ragan, Cynthia, and I can spend sixteen to eighteen hours a day together and still come out laughing. Like the *Peanuts* cartoon, "Happiness is . . ." intimacy is:

> Being in Glorieta, New Mexico, when Cynthia double-dog-dared Ragan to shave off his beard *and* moustache, and he *did!*
>
> Being mutually excited about returning to a hotel that serves a baked potato that's a "10";
>
> Sharing together some of your most embarrassing moments in performances (like the time I tripped off the platform and fell flat on my face in front of the congregation at First Baptist Church, Fayetteville, Arkansas);
>
> Being caught childishly giggling about the same thing in a Sunday morning worship service;
>
> Knowing by the look in Cynthia's eyes that, yes, she *is* going to bring her dog on stage to sing with her!

Then, there was the time that:

> After a concert in El Paso, we went with several friends to Juarez to find some "great Mexican food" only to have to settle for Chinese food at Don's because it was the only decent place open after 10:00 PM,
>
> Or when we flew into Gulfport, Mississippi, at 8:30 on a Saturday night and discovered that the airline had once again lost all our luggage. We had an early Sunday morning TV appearance to make, so Ragan "convinced" the airline to give each of us an allowance for clothes and makeup. We rushed to a mall, and in the last five minutes that Sears was open we each bought an outfit, shoes, and makeup for $50! (I won't say how long ago that was!)
>
> *Note from Mother:* To add to Patti's story—my cousin, James Moore, declares he will never forget that night. He had met them at the airport and far exceeded the speed limit in driving them to Sears. He laughs and tells how he held the door open and watched

them simply gobble up their purchases. Later, much to Ragan's dismay as he was dressing the next morning, he discovered that he had picked up a size 18 shirt instead of his size 15.

Patti

The truest mark of the intimacy we all share came in November of 1983 with a midnight phone call to Nashville. Nineteen eighty-three was "The Year That Was" for many, and Scott and I were not left unaffected.

We had been struggling financially with Scott's building a new dental office and my starting a new business. We were both growing weary from two or three years of traumatic changes in our families' lives, and the battle increased to the degree that we were daily struggling to survive— emotionally and mentally, as well as financially.

By October I cracked under the weight of several years' burdens, was hospitalized for two weeks, and released to private therapy, only to return to the hospital two weeks later. Scott and I both were going to a Christian doctor for counseling, and many prayers for us were being lifted up by hundreds of friends all over the States.

The road to healing began when I called Cynthia and Ragan and gave the news, "We don't know what we're going to do, but Scott is closing his office and we're packing up the house. We know we're supposed to leave San Antonio, but we have nowhere to go."

Ragan confidently and assuringly suggested, "Yes, you do, Patti! You and Scott and Matt come here and stay with us. We're family. You tell Scott that we'll work through this."

We could not begin to envision how the Lord had already begun to work and how He would once again use Cynthia's concerts to produce miraculous blessings. We were already living temporarily in Nashville when Scott received a phone call from Dr. Ron Weaks of Greenville, Texas. "I met your sister-in-law at a concert this week," he said, "and I'm interested in talking with you about working with me in my dental practice."

The ways the Lord worked during those weeks in our lives could fill a book in itself. But once again I could praise the Lord when I sang:

He saw me, He saw me and reached out His hand.

He loved me. Why He loved me, I can't understand.
He lifted—He lifted me up from my feet.
And I'll thank Him in Heaven when face to face we meet.

Back to Virginia: A bond had been drawn many years before the girls became aware of it, or it would not be as binding as it is in their adult years. They had become the sisters I had longed to have all my life.

This bond was apparent as I read their contributions to this chapter. In the months past, when they were together they would talk about what they could write about for "Mama's book," but when they finally wrote they were miles apart. Patti was in Greenville, Texas, and Cynthia in Nashville, Tennessee. Yet, in so many ways their stories "dovetail" one another, since they have recalled separately the experiences and recollections of the past. The bond ties their lives and hearts together.

Cynthia

My sister and I are bound by more than mere genetic similarities. We have years of joint experiences. As children we fought like cats and . . . cats. Mother often would resort to spankings in order to try to transform two wild felines into sweet, docile house cats. Sometimes she was reduced to tears as she exclaimed, "How could two sisters treat each other the way you do? Don't you even love each other?" Had either of us dared to answer then it would have been a resounding, "No, ma'am!"

People often drove wedges between us without ever realizing it. Patti was *always* the pretty one, the little doll, the blue-eyed blonde and all the men flattered and flirted with her even as a baby. They never flirted with me, and how it galled me! She, on the other hand, must have been equally galled by the fact that some people saw me as a cross between Jenny Lind and Mary, the mother of Jesus. I was the good one—mind you, not pretty, simply good. Little did they know I would have sold my soul to hear one compliment concerning my physical appearance. The only thing I do remember vividly to this day was a comment by my father. "Cynthia, you have my legs. Legs like a football player," he teased me one day. Couldn't he have even used "dancer"?

So at an early age the battle lines were drawn: Saint Joan versus Jean Harlow? And *I* had to be the saint!

Daddy was, I am now glad to write, a strict father. As a conservative Baptist he understood and was quick to remind us that the depravity of man was evident in his children. *He's so right,* I thought, *especially as far as Patti is concerned!* We were sisters in the battle. We battled over bathroom rights, hand-me-downs, eyebrow pencils (the only makeup we were allowed to wear for years), and horror of horrors, head lice.

We were living in Pleasanton, Texas, where our daddy was the pastor of the First Baptist Church. Patti and I, with some of the girls from the church, spent a Friday night in an old bunk house in the country. We giggled, laughed, had pillow fights, and hardly slept. That next Saturday night when Mother was washing our hair she screamed.

"Tommy, come here! Oh, dear gussie, what is this in the girls' hair?" Being a teacher in public schools for years, she knew exactly what was in our heads—lice! What to do was a major problem. Late Saturday night in Pleasanton there were no drug stores open to obtain any medicine, shampoo, poison, or whatever one finds to kill lice. That was just as well. Had they been open, Mother would have physically restrained the first person to try to step outside the house. You see, if anyone had gone for help they would have, in effect, announced to the whole community that we were filthy white trash. So Mother repeatedly wet our hair in heavy mineral oil, and began combing dead bugs from our hair, bugs dead from asphyxiation. She combed frantically on into the night. Then using a shampoo that smelled like sheep dip, she shampooed and shampooed our hair. The lice were dead, and we were nearly dead ourselves, but the oil was still thick in our hair. Our hair was much more stubborn than the bugs.

The next morning we *had* to go to church. Neither parent even thought for a moment that we could miss going to church for such a petty excuse as wet, oily hair. Mother rolled our hair in pin curls and tied our heads up in scarves that made us look like small, pale versions of Hattie McDaniels playing Mammy in *Gone with the Wind.*

Humiliated beyond expression, Patti and I sat meekly in Sunday School reeking of sheep dip. Mother advised, "Girls, tell them your hair didn't dry." This was true, since mineral oil does not dry, and we were living in the days before hair dryers. "And if either of you raises a finger to your head," she continued, "I will spank you when we get home!" There was a demented, near-hysterical look in her eyes, like a woman possessed, that told us she was deadly serious. Somehow we survived, and we never told anyone about the lice. And the other girls who went to the bunk house that fateful night *never* asked us why our hair was rolled up and in a scarf that day, nor did we ever ask them if they too had been infected.

But those lice and those oily head scarves united me and Patti and Hawthorne's heroine Hester Prynne in the mute fellowship of public humiliation. I never did ask why we could not have simply stayed home and not attended church that morning. Somehow in those days it was not an option. We were always in church unless we were in bed with a high fever. I was a grown, married woman before I ever saw the end of *The Wizard of Oz*. We always left for Training Union (now Church Training) during that delightful, fanciful movie, so I never was able to see the ending. That is how life was then. I wish they were now.

When I left for college Patti and I turned into best friends, it seems, overnight! The fighting was finally over. A point of truce was our music. Both of us had been carefully nurtured in the faith and in the music of that faith. We studied music—piano at first, and then we were both in high school bands. In college we both majored in music. In church we often did the special music; Patti played and I sang. I had been singing for as long as I can remember, and when Patti accompanied me it was with such sensitivity that we seemed one. Indeed, we were one in the Spirit. Her piano supported me, surrounded me like an orchestra.

After college and a brief stint in Hollywood doing a summer replacement for CBS, I made some decisions that most people would think were foolish. I turned down jobs, agents, and living in Los Angeles to go back to Texas. I had this impression that somehow God wanted me to go home again. In spite of the fact that there are those who say you can never go home again, I did. I moved to Dallas where I got a job singing jingles. Patti joined me, and we found ourselves traveling around the country singing in churches. I never planned to be a "gospel singer." I was simply a Christian who was a singer. I found my faith being revealed as a natural extension of who I was. I sang an evening concert with a wide variety of musical styles and lyrics, but woven in and through the concert would be a definite witness to my heritage and my love of the Lord Jesus. In those days Christians did not boo you off the platform like they do today. I felt free then to express my art as fully as I was able with my "family," the Christians in Baptist churches.

It was years before I was to sing in a church of another denomination. I was relieved to find music broke down denominational boundaries. I still struggle for that earlier freedom. It is a gift, not without price, and not so readily given to Christian artists today. Christian painters don't have to paint churches only, and Christian electricians don't wire denominational buildings only. Why do Christian singers have to be limited to singing only church songs? Forgive me, as I rise to the level of a low soapbox. The truth is I sing about Jesus because that is the most natural thing I can do with my art. I think, however, He must enter and minister and heal in every aspect of our lives. And music is simply a tool that lets people be exposed to Him and His Word. I, at my most supreme moments, am simply an instrument He uses.

As Patti and I went about the countryside making music we had so many experiences that could have upset or frustrated us. We had to rely a good deal on the sense of humor we seemed to have inherited from our parents and grandparents. "Just as soon laugh as cry," my grandmother often opined, and we did both. I recall one weekend in particular.

We were young, fancy-free, and, we hoped, glamorous. My car was loaded with suitcases, and a clothes rack across the back seat held our formal gowns (for concerts) that Mama had made. This particular weekend Patti and I were traveling to a church southwest of Houston. It was the time of year when it rained heavily in the coastal areas of Texas, and the rain was torrential. My car didn't have too many miles on it, so we never had any car trouble on the road. Therefore, I felt secure driving the car at a fast clip. (This was before fifty-five miles-per-hour speed limits.)

That evening we were late, so we were traveling dressed for the performance. Suddenly, in the pouring rain, a sickening thud-thud-thud told us we had a flat tire. Dressed fully formal and frightened, we pulled over on the side of the road. We had no idea what to do! Where was a filling station? Where were other cars? Where were the state troopers when you needed them? We resorted to the one source of help most Christians resort to when there is no other choice. We began to pray.

"Lord, we need your help! Please send someone to rescue us and get us to the church on time." No sooner had we prayed that an old, beat-up car pulled up beside us on the road. It was hard to see through the steamed windows of our car and the night rain into the dark car next to us. Our faith was weak ("trembling" at that point, you might say) when we rolled down the window and saw a dark face peering at us, asking, "You girls need help?" I wanted to scream, "No!" Stories of murder and rape on lonely country roads rushed to the front of my mind. "What'll we do, Patti?" I asked. She began to laugh nervously, "Don't unlock the doors."

"Well, we *can't* sit here all night," I offered, even though I would rather have done so than what I did next. I opened my door. "Don't leave me!" squealed Patti as she slipped across the front seat and out my door right behind me.

"Can I help you girls?" the black man smiled.

"Yes, I think you can. We need to get to the First Baptist Church," I said, as I scooted across his front seat. Patti was pushing right behind me, clinging to me in apprehension. If this stranger were an ax murderer, he could surely strike two victims with one blow, we were so close. As I reached to pick up some papers I was sitting on, I noticed that the papers were tracts, the kind that are often handed out on street corners by zealous Christians. A quick survey of the old car revealed an old, beat-up Bible, apparently well read.

What relief! Our quick prayer of desperation for help had sent a black minister who was doing some visitation that dark, rainy night. And like a knight of old, in dented armor, he delivered us to the front door of the First Baptist Church—damp, disheveled, and determined to be more trusting in God hearing our prayers.

The next day found us laughing our way two hundred miles to Beaumont, Texas. In spite of all of the fussing and fighting Patti and I did as young sisters, we never had a cross word on the road. She became my protector and defender and would fight a whole roomful of dragons for me if the need arose. She seemed to equate anything that ruffled my feathers with a mortal enemy. There were those times in concerts when we were both intensely aware of spiritual battles being fought around us. And always when we began to sing, we were aware of the Holy Spirit's leading; and even though we had a program planned and written out, I would sometimes feel impressed to change our direction or message. Patti was right there picking up my thoughts as I subtly led us to change our program.

Patti and I "went from town to town and village to village proclaiming the good news of the kingdom of God." I, for a period, thought God might be leading me into foreign missions. After all, what vocational choices were open to women in the late 1960s who felt "called"? I feel had Daddy thought God had called Patti and me to preach, we would have both wound up like Jeptha's daughter—dead! But he could accept our proclaiming the Word, if it was dressed in music. And that was what we did. We both accepted the Great Commission in Matthew 28:19-20 as a command directed at us personally. Years later I realized that it is a personal commission to *every* believer. We had no career designs as far as gospel music was concerned. We simply went where we were invited.

Oh, the innocence of the good old days! Later agents and managers showed us that "all of this could be ours if we would only. . . ." After a brief journey down that road we won some awards, but they were hollow. As nice as it is to be given the approval of the world in the form of little statuettes and plaques, and to go to lavish parties, be driven in chauffeured limousines, and hear the applause when your name is called out as the winner, I hereby testify that it is all merely treasure here on earth. The only time an award mattered to me was the time I gave one away.

It was Christmas, and our family had enlarged from our original five to twenty-two (counting Ragan's side). Patti had heard of a family that had given one another something they already had that was meaningful to them, and would be meaningful to the recipient. It was not an expensive Christmas that year, but it was deeply moving.

Mama gave Ragan a framed poem by Emily Dickinson, his favorite American poet. She gave me some of her costume jewelry that I had admired since I was a child. Daddy and Mama made unique toys for all of the grandchildren. The men exchanged twenty-year-old, out-of-style ties that brought riotous laughter. I gave Patti an award I had received from the Gospel Music Association for singing. I had been surprised when I won it, but I felt it was in no way mine. It was God's award—God's and the people in my life who were His instruments. It belonged to Daddy, who taught me always to seek to serve my Lord; it belonged to Mama who introduced me to the piano and taught me to love it even in my young childhood; it belonged to Ragan, my husband, who supported me as he encouraged me to write music; it belonged to Buryl Red, whose artistry and friendship have proven the test of time; it belonged to George Gagliardi and Raymond Brown, who gave to me so generously their songs; it belonged to my denomination, which nurtured and encouraged me to use my gifts and talents; it belonged to Sarah Baker, my college vocal teacher, who gave me strength and technique and encouragement; and it belonged to Patti, who had been my fellow soldier in the battle, my orchestra, my truest friend, my sister in every sense of that beautiful word.

When she picked up her package she started weeping even before she opened it. I am fully aware that my whole family is intensely emotional and outrageously dramatic, but I was still surprised to look around the living room and see all the adults weeping. Why was that such an emotional moment? It had been a difficult year for all of us—a year of stepping out on faith, knowing that our faith was no more than a thin sheet of ice over a deep ocean. Some of us had seen that thin layer of faith crack and break. We could have drifted off on our own ice floes, but something held us together. Something bound us as a family. Something tied us even closer than blood. That something is so wonderful that the only way I can express it is in song. That something is none other than God's love for us.

The present I gave Patti was finally coming full circle. It was truly hers all along. We all wept that night out of a deep love for one another, for God, and for our high calling, and from joy. Yes, we wept for joy. And we ended that Christmas celebration singing like we have done for as long as I can remember.

There's no friend like a sister!

8

God Leads His
Dear Children Along

Some thro' the waters, some thro' the flood,
Some thro' the fire, but all thro' the Blood;
Some thro' great sorrow, but God gives a song,
In the night season and all the day long.[19]

It is easy to sing praises unto the Lord, giving thanks for all things when the day is bright and cheery and all things seem to be going *our* way. But what about the night hours—the times when we feel forsaken, forgotten by God, can we sing our song then? Can we praise His name for all things? We can if our attitude is like that of the psalmist in Psalm 77:6: "I call to remembrance my song in the night."

"God Leads His Dear Children Along," sometimes through the darkest of nights when the last light has gone out and fear stalks in, and hope runs away and hides.

In Psalm 137, we read the captive's cry from a dark night in the lives of the children of Judah. They had been carried captive far from their homes and into a strange land. "By the rivers of Babylon, there we sat down; yea, we wept, when we remembered Zion. We hung our harps upon the willows in the midst thereof. For there they that carried us away captive required of us a song . . .; saying, Sing us one of the songs of Zion. How shall we sing the Lord's song in a [foreign] land?" (vv. 1-4).

Our "foreign land" might be discord, grief, uncertainty, and frustrations, but our Heavenly Father can bring us into a land of melody, if we can only trust Him, knowing that He works *all* things out for our good and His glory (Rom. 8:28).

118

Several years ago, night descended upon us in the form of a car accident involving our son, Tombo, his best friend Steve Downum, and Steve's sister Ruthie. The boys were both fifteen and Ruthie was eighteen.

It had been a beautiful spring day in San Antonio, and a typical Sunday morning service, the first following a fantastic spiritual lift through a revival in our church. Ruthie had been in her usual place at the organ and I at the piano. I remember later that night, when I looked at that battered face, thinking how angelic she had looked that morning in her pretty, baby-pink dress.

Tombo had asked to go home with Stevie after the service, and I told him to be sure and get his jeans, because I knew the boys would spend the biggest part of the afternoon traipsing over the fields of the farm. The boys had known each other since they were little but had been close friends only for a couple of years since the Downums had joined our church. They had much in common, both being preacher's "kids," each loving to sing, and both were leaders among the young people in our church. Leroy, Steve's dad, is chaplain at the Texas State Chest Hospital and had pastored several churches in and around San Antonio before going into the chaplaincy.

About 4 in the afternoon, Brother Tom came into the bedroom where I was resting and said, "For some reason God wants me to change the evening message. I can't get away from it." This was most unusual, for after giving his Sunday messages much thought and prayer throughout the week, he seldom if ever changed his mind about the messages.

Picking up the newspaper that was lying on the bed and starting to write, he said, "Let me give you the outline."

He never got to preach that sermon—God had given it just for our hearts. God was saying—oh, so gently—"I've picked out a valley for you" to go through, but "I'll be with you." In less than two hours we were in that valley.

God prepares us for all things. With His great omniscience He knows what lies ahead and wants to be a buffer for the problems that arise, for the lessons we must learn.

It was nearing the time for youth choir practice, and the kids would soon be returning to town. Ruthie had been visiting some of their cousins and had gone home to pick up the boys. A short distance from the house something happened to the truck (we will never know just what—the truck was totaled). Possibly the A-frame dropped or the steering mechanism failed. Ruthie was unable to steer in a straight line.

The truck hit a concrete bridge, leveling fifteen feet of concrete and steel but managed to remain upright. Everything under the hood was jammed into the cab.

We were notified within a few minutes after the wreck, and not knowing what we would find at the hospital, we literally flew through the streets of San Antonio, praying that the children would be all right. *Perhaps they had been taken to the hospital only for observation,* we kept telling ourselves.

Running through the doors of the emergency entrance and down the long hall, we could hear Tombo screaming, "Get me out of here! Get me out of here!"

As we ran into that strange, antiseptic room, where a male nurse was forcefully holding him on the gurney, we heard him singing, "I was born to serve the Lord. . . ." In his delirium, he still had a song!

His head was opened from his right eye to the back of his head, and we saw bone sticking into his brain. How could our boy live? How could he be singing in this "foreign land"?

Through the late evening hours and into the morning, the doctors worked on the three young people. There was so much to do, so many injuries, so many X-rays to determine the extent of each one. Ruthie remained alert and could talk to us, but she could not remember what had happened. In fact, the last memory she had was that of picking the boys up at the house.

On first examination, Steve seemed to be hurt the least, but he was so quiet. Then it became apparent that his head injury needed immediate attention as his hemoglobin dropped. They had taken Tombo into the operating room by then to begin their work on him, but believing that he would not make it anyway, they turned to Steve and began to do what they could for him.

After the surgery on both boys was complete, we asked the doctor what chance our son had, and he merely shook his head. Not wanting to build up our hopes, he quietly answered, "Well, if he makes it through the night, he has a better chance."

In the intensive care waiting room at the Baptist Memorial Hospital, the entire south wall is filled with windows, but if you stand far down at the southwest corner in the early hours of morning and look toward the east, you can see the break of day. You know where we were standing that morning! As we saw the first pencil line that appeared along the eastern horizon, hope rose in our hearts as we gave thanks that our son had come through the night. For nine long mornings, we stood hand in hand, looking for the dawn, because each night the doctors would simply repeat, "If he makes it through the night."

Several years later when I heard someone sing, "Joy Comes in the Morning," I once again lived those anxious nights and thought how true it is that "weeping only lasts for the night." God gives us a promise when He says through the songwriter:

> Hold on, my child.
> Joy comes in the morning.
> The darkest hour means dawn is just in sight.[20]

Light does bring hope!

Cynthia and Patti were in Hobbs, New Mexico, that night in concert. When we finally reached them by phone, Cynthia asked, "Daddy, is it bad?" and he replied, "Just come home as quickly as you can and hang onto Romans 8:28."

Cynthia told us later that they had gone to their motel room to wait for a private plane which would fly them to Lubbock, where they could catch a commercial flight. They had clung to each other and cried, knowing it must be bad if their daddy had said to hang onto that verse.

Morning came. The boys were still alive, Ruthie was resting, and we knew that God had given us a few more hours. The girls arrived about noon, and when Cynthia went in to see Tommy, he spoke to her, and they sang all four verses of "Amazing Grace" together while the doctors and nurses in the intensive care room stood by with tears in their eyes. Of course, Tombo doesn't remember this, for it was nine days before he was fully conscious.

God's amazing grace carried us through the days that followed—through a tracheotomy surgery for Ruthie, through Steve's death on Wednesday night (he never made a sound after he was brought to the hospital), surgery again for Tombo on Thursday night to remove his spleen, and then, Steve's funeral on Saturday.

In Tombo's delirium, he must have had many worries and anxieties, for he called for so many of his friends and family members.

He had been chosen for the All-City Junior High Band and was second chair drummer. His friend, William Myers, was first chair, and the spring concert was to be that week. Tombo kept saying, "Tell William I don't think I can make the concert."

Then he really had the nurses puzzled—he kept calling for Hilda and making kissing sounds with his lips. One time when we were beside his bed, one of the nurses whispered, "I feel so sorry for him. He keeps calling for his girl friend."

We laughed and told her that was his dachshund. One of the members in our church said, "If I thought I could get by with it, I'd bring Hilda to the hospital in a basket."

Tombo constantly called for Steve, not knowing that he was in the bed next to him the first three nights. On the fifth night, they had returned Tombo to surgery to save his life once again, for the spleen had been ruptured in the wreck, but his other injuries were too serious for him to stand that operation on Sunday night.

Brother Tom explained to Tombo what they were going to do, and because Tombo was so distraught over Steve and had been asking so many questions that day, Tom said, "Son, I don't want you to ask any more questions. Just relax so the doctors can do their job. We'll talk about it all later."

The doctors had advised us not to tell Tombo or Ruthie of Steve's death, but when on the ninth day Tombo was removed from ICU and placed in a semiprivate room, Brother Tom decided not to heed the doctor's advice and to tell him, because we did not want him to hear it accidentally. So, Tom cleared the room and gently began to tell Tombo what had happened. He explained, "Son, you know we've all been praying for the three of you. Possibly you've had more prayers going up to heaven for you than anyone else ever had. (We received letters, calls, and telegrams from people all over the world. There were prayer meetings in a nondenominational church in Denver, a Congregational Church in Connecticut, a Mennonite church in California, Baptist churches all over Texas and other states, a group of missionaries in the Bahamas, a prayer group on the *USS Kitty Hawk* in the waters of Vietnam, and on the *USS Enterprise*. A Catholic school in our neighborhood had daily prayer over the intercom, and the school Ruthie and Steve attended on the outskirts of San Antonio prayed daily.) You know, Son, the Downums and Mother and I have prayed that all three of you would live, but only if you were going to be healed and returned to your normal health. God in His love and mercy has taken Stevie home."

Tom waited for the shock to pass and watched Tombo with love and much concern. Tombo looked up, through glistening tears, and asked, "Why couldn't I go with Stevie?"

His daddy answered, "Son, we don't know the answer to that, but for some reason, some purpose, God has seen fit to leave you here with us. And we praise Him for that, but now you have a responsibility to find out what that purpose is."

We learned more about God's grace during this "dark night" of our lives than we had ever known; how God sustains us when hope is gone, when grief seems too heavy to bear, when fears overwhelm us. We asked what "good" thing could come of this night? How could God bring anything good out of this chaos, this tragedy, this loss of a vibrant young life about to blossom into manhood, our son whose body from the waist up was so mutilated and torn. But in the days, weeks, and even years that followed, we have found some answers. Souls were born into God's kingdom, lives were touched by the testimonies of the two families, and our church was strengthened and drawn into a closer-knit family.

Shortly before the accident, Brother Tom was asked to submit a sermon for the "sermon of the week" in the *San Antonio Light* newspaper. The Lord gave him a message and he called it, "Bright Assurances for Dark Days." The editor changed the title to "Doom Can't Stifle God's Vow," and it appeared in the newspaper the Saturday after the accident, the day Steve was buried. Many people thought Tom had written it during the week because it was so apropos.

Using Micah 4:9-10 as his text, Brother Tom quoted from a poem he had found in his files written by Wilhelmina Stitch:

> My lamp is shattered, and so dark that night;
> My lamp is shattered, yet to my glad sight—
>   a star shines on.
>
> My lamp is shattered, but a star shines bright,
>   and by its glowing I can wend aright.
> My lamp is shattered, but I still can fight—
>   for a star shines on.
>
> My lamp is shattered, sad indeed my plight,
> My lamp is shattered, yet I'll reach the height—
>   for a star shines on.[21]

Quoted from the sermon: "In Micah, we find a message of doom and defeat—Jerusalem's streets would be downtrodden by her enemies. The city is to become a pile of rubble—the site of the Temple will be like a forest.

"But like 'stars that shine on' are some wonderful truths from God's Word that, even in the midst of this message of doom, come as bright assurances for dark days that will help us when it seems that all is lost and that no one cares."

Two weeks after the wreck, Wanda, one of the girls from the youth group in our church, came forward accepting Christ as her Savior and asking if she might say something to the church. I had been Wanda's Sunday School teacher when she was a sixth grader, and I knew what courage was required for her to come down the aisle. She was shy and reticent about speaking in public.

With tears streaming down her face, she testified, "You know, I got mad at God when Stevie died, for he was one of the best in our group. Why did God have to take him? And then I got to thinking—Stevie was a good Christian, and if that had been me, I wouldn't go to heaven, because I'm not really a Christian."

A life for a life, and God still works things out for our good. This doesn't mean we will understand His methods, nor will we know all He has in store for us, but inevitable good will come from it to glorify God.

Answers are still coming, and it has been thirteen years since that fateful night. A couple of years ago, Brother Tom was holding a revival at the Northridge Park Baptist Church in San Antonio. On the first night he noticed a man singing in the choir who seemed to shine with the love of God in his very being. He was standing on the back row, alone, and as Brother Tom watched him, he could see why he was back there—he sang with every part of his body, as if his voice alone was not enough to give to the One he was worshiping.

One night that week Tombo visited in the service, and when Brother Tom introduced him, he spoke of the wreck. Many of the people in the congregation remembered those days in our lives, as all of San Antonio had, for it had hit the headlines for several reasons.

The morning after the accident, one of the radio announcers had said, "I want you to know that San Antonio is a town of love. This morning there are two of our families waiting anxiously beside the beds of their children after that major accident last night. People from all over the city came last night to wait with the families. It is estimated that between 200-250 people clogged the halls of the hospital waiting and praying with their friends. (Later it was estimated that there were at least forty to fifty ministers from all denominations who came to the hospital after their evening services had ended.) San Antonio is a city that cares for her own!"

The road on which the accident occurred had been a source of controversy for some years—as to whose responsibility it was to widen those narrow 1920 bridges. There had been several deaths from other accidents on that road since we had moved to San Antonio. Another petition was signed and taken to the legislature in Austin that week—the bridges were fixed.

So, the congregation that night did remember.

Afterwards, the "joyous singer" came up and asked, "Did that happen about 1970-71?"

Brother Tom said, "Yes, in April of 1971. Why?"

"I knew it, I knew it," he said excitedly. "I was that service man whose mother-in-law was in ICU when those young people were brought in that night. You people took time out to ask about us and care for our loved one. I couldn't get over that—we were strangers. And all those friends of yours came that night and kept coming all week!"

"I'll never forget the night that boy died, when his father stood up on that chair and said, "Brother Tom, would you come and lead us in a prayer of thanksgiving for Steve has just gone Home.

"You know, I could never get away from the knowledge that you folks had something I didn't have. A couple of years went by, and one day I was driving my truck when the Lord kept speaking to me—and you know what I did? I just stopped that truck, got out, and knelt down in the road beside my truck, and said, 'Lord, I'm yours if you'll have me.' "

Another life added to the kingdom—God works all things together.

Ruthie and Tombo, both grown now, each have their own families. The doctors in San Antonio just shake their heads with amazement as they look at these living miracles.

> You ask me why my heart keeps singing
> Why I can sing when things go wrong
> But since I've found the source of music
> I just can't help it
> God gave the song.[22]

As I look back along our pilgrim journey, I think that the 1970s were some of the greatest years of our lives and some of the darkest nights. Until then, our family had been blessed with good health; the children had suffered only the usual childhood diseases; I still had my parents and Brother Tom had his mother; and there had been a minimum number of deaths in our extended families. Thus, the Lord had some lessons He wanted us to learn and some experiences we had to pass through in order to be better ministers of His love and grace.

Many times we had stood with a friend beside the casket of the most precious person in their lives and consoled, "I understand what you're going through," but really we didn't because we had not walked that road before.

It wasn't until December, 1973—when my father, William Byron Wilbanks, died—that I realized what an empty phrase that could be unless you too have been there. Now I know and can have genuine empathy, and not just sympathy, for someone who is experiencing a crushing sorrow.

After the loss in death of that special person in your life, the nights drag on for a long time, seemingly never to end, but you can have consolation in knowing that we do not have to walk alone; others have already been there, others are experiencing the same anguish and despair. There is solace in realizing that our Lord Jesus walked through such a night when word came of the illness and then death of his dear friend Lazarus (John 11:1-44).

When word came that my father had died after only a week's illness, we made plans to go immediately. I had seen him in the middle of the week but had to return to my teaching job, so I was not there that Sunday morning.

Cynthia called while we were making preparations. She was in California in concert and told us that she had just called her grandmother to check on "Papaw," only to find that he had just passed away. She said, "I want to sing. The Lord led me to sing an old hymn in the concert and now I know why—it was for Papaw."

> When peace, like a river, attendeth my way,
> When sorrows like sea billows roll;
> Whatever my lot, thou hast taught me to say,
> It is well, it is well with my soul.[23]

Dark clouds were still near, for even with the burial of my father the week before Christmas, this night did not end.

Cynthia had recently announced her engagement to Ragan Courtney in November, and plans were under way for a February wedding. Ragan's mother, Sybil, after fighting a long battle with cancer, died the week after Christmas.

With those two deaths, plans were canceled for an elaborate wedding.

I remember a chorus Brother Tom and I used to sing when we were young:

> He sends the rainbow, a lovely rainbow,
> He sends the rainbow with the rain. . . .[24]

And truly He does. Their wedding was the rainbow we needed at such a time—a luscious valley between two mountains we had crossed. And there was still another mountain ahead, and we were unaware of it.

In a few months, we were to gain another son-in-law since Patti planned a June wedding. Patti was married, and this was the last time we were to see my brother, Zene Wilbanks, until the first of November. Through the years we had been a close-knit family—my folks, my brother, his family, and ours. We shared holidays and vacation times, and kept in contact in between.

It wasn't unusual, though, for two or three months to pass without our seeing each other because of our jobs. So, when he called late that October night, it dawned on us that we had not been together since the wedding.

He seemed agitated and upset; my first thought was *Mother,* for she had been having a lonesome time since father's death. With tears in his voice, he said, "I guess you would like to know that I'm an outpatient at M. D. Anderson."

Brother Tom and I, both on the extension phones, were shocked, and Tom said what I couldn't voice—"What has happened, Zene?"

He had received a report from the doctor on some everyday-type X-rays he had taken—two spots on the upper lung and several in the lymph glands. In less than six weeks he was gone—the quickest time we had ever known for a cancer patient.

He was a man in perfect health only a few months before. In fact, because of this, the doctors asked if they could use an experimental kind of chemotherapy that could only be administered to someone in good physical condition. He readily agreed, and they had to fly the medicine and a doctor into Houston. So, perhaps they made a new discovery in the long struggle to combat cancer. We pray for this.

We buried Zene on December 8, lacking ten days being exactly one year since my father was laid to rest. I had not really grieved—sorrowed, yes—over my father's death, for I understood that was how he would have wanted to go; he had led a full, long life, had seen his children grown and with families, and had watched his six grandchildren grow up. But this death was different.

Zene was only forty-four years old, so young, so talented, with so much still to give his family and the world. He was a musician, an artist, and had the kind of personality that drew young and old to him. He had given of himself to many of the young people of his community through the Little League and the South Houston High School.

When his daughters were in the pep squad, he had carved little Trojan figurines out of wood for each of them. He had sat on the bench with the football boys, encouraging them, congratulating them in all their victories, weeping in their defeats. At his funeral, the entire football team and all the coaches filed into the church as one group.

Though he was only three years my junior, I had always affectionately thought of him as my "baby" brother. Brother Tom called him "Little Brother," and to some this seemed incongruous since Zene stood a good three inches taller than he.

In the months that followed his funeral, I began to grieve like I never dreamed I would. The tears were never far away. Many times even at school, I would have to walk out into the hallway, rather than let my children see their teacher crying.

I felt ashamed, because hadn't I always talked to others in their grief and shared how God is able to take away the pain, if we only would let Him? And here I wasn't able to take my own advice.

Remember the old cliché, "The Lord often puts us on our backs so we can look up"? Well, He put me on the floor. One morning at school, while the children were outside in PE, I pushed a child's chair up to the wall and stood on it to finish decorating the bulletin board for the month of March. I was busy working when the art teacher came in to ask a question. I answered, "I don't know, but let me finish this, and we'll go to the office to find out."

Before I knew it I was on the floor, on my right side with my arm pinned under me. She implored, "Oh, Mrs. Clawson, are you all right?"

Trying to gather my thoughts, I replied, "Yes, but help me up. I've broken my arm." How I knew that, I don't really know. At the same time, I somehow knew that everything was going to be all right and felt an unusual presence of the Lord. It was as if He was hovering over me like a tent; as if He were saying, "I don't want you to hurt, but this is for your good." I had never experienced anything like it before.

The elbow was dislocated, and one of the bones in the forearm was chipped. The doctor frightened me when he said, "A few more ounces of pressure, and the arm would have been ruined." But the Lord knows exactly how far He must take us for complete healing. The shots the doctor had given made me severely ill, so my principal suggested that I take the rest of the week off.

We were preparing to go to Nashville for "Praise Sing," the introduction of the new *Baptist Hymnal,* on Friday of that week. The whole family was to be there, since Ragan was one of the authors in the hymnal, and Cynthia and Patti were to give a concert on Wednesday night. We left San Antonio as planned, and I believe I was the only one in 10,000 at the colosseum with a broken arm.

On Wednesday night, before the girls were to give their concert, Jeanie C. Riley blessed our hearts when she sang and gave her testimony. Then, Myrtle Hall began her concert.

I have always loved to hear her sing and was drinking it all in. After a brief testimony, she began singing a song I had not heard. Later, when I tried to explain what had taken place in my heart and soul, I could only describe that it seemed like "hands pulling cobwebs out of my mind."

I sensed that it was far more than that, for as I listened to that song, tears began to flow down my cheeks, the burden was lifted, the grief and sorrow were gone, and I was free. God was working His mighty will in me, and I knew why He had to get my attention so dramatically. I grabbed Brother Tom's arm and whispered, "I've been healed! It's all gone—the grief!" And he understood what I meant.

After we returned to the hotel that night, I was trying to remember the name of the song Myrtle had sung, but I couldn't. None of the rest of the family seemed to recall it either. I shrugged, "Oh, well, it was just what I needed, anyway."

A couple of weeks after we returned home, Tombo showed me a piece of sheet music, saying, "Mama, this is the song that Myrtle was singing in Nashville. I just found it among all that music we picked up there."

As I reread the lines, I knew why it had spoken to me. The song was written by Dan Burgess, and I want to give you the words, so perhaps it will be the instrument for some healing that needs to take place in your life.

"I Thank You, Lord"

Thank you, Lord, for the trials that come my way,
In that way I can grow each day as I let you lead.
And thank You, Lord, for the patience those trials bring,
In that process of growing I can learn to care.

But it goes against the way I am to put my human
    nature down,
And let the Spirit take control of all I do.
'Cause when those trials come, my human nature shouts
    the thing to do,
And God's soft prompting can be easily ignored.

I thank You, Lord, with each trial I feel inside,
That you're there to help lead and guide me away
    from wrong.
'Cause You promised, Lord, that with ev'ry testing
That Your way of escaping is easier to bear.

I thank You, Lord, for the vic'try that growing brings,
In surrender of ev'rything, life is so worthwhile.
And I thank You, Lord, that when ev'rything's put
    in place
Out in front I can see Your face and it's there You
    belong.[25]

Today, as I read that first line of the chorus again—"It goes against the way I am to put my human nature down"—I realize that without being aware of it, I was trying to work out the grief in my own power, and not taking hold of the power the Lord was offering. Why we waste our time, and the Lord's, with our self-important styles, I don't know, when "[His] way of escaping is easier to bear."

But there are griefs far worse than death. Death is final. We miss our loved ones, but as time passes the memory dims, and our pain becomes more distant.

The fall of 1974 ushered in one of the darkest nights. When your child is hurting and there is nothing you can do, there is a pain that cannot be doctored with a pain-killing pill.

From the beginning of Patti's marriage in June 1973, trouble signs developed like warning lights. We could see their unhappiness, but really didn't worry too much, for outwardly they had everything that could make for a healthy marriage. We thought they were having to make some adjustments as all newlyweds do.

As the months went by, it became apparent that they were not going to work out their problems, so Patti left and visited some friends in Corpus Christi who had been like a second set of parents to her. She wrote us, asking if she could come home. We called her immediately upon receiving the letter and assured her that we would meet the plane when she came. Yes, of course, she could come home. We wanted to help.

There followed some of the blackest nights in our relationship with our child, as we all tried to work through this valley.

> Tho' sorrows befall us, and Satan oppose,
> God leads his dear children along,
> Through grace we can conquer, defeat all our foes,
> God leads His dear children along.

Patti was devastated. Our first thought was, "Where have we failed as parents?" and guilt took over. Then, the hurt came because we could not help to alleviate the pain Patti was suffering, and so more guilt fell on our shoulders. It became a vicious circle because Patti didn't want to bring pain to us, either. Satan really had a heyday.

Then, through the love and caring of friends and the beloved people of our church, God began the healing. I wish it had come overnight, but the nights stretched out into years for all of us. However, for us as parents, God began to show how we could become better servants even through this. Once again in the schoolhouse of life, He was the Teacher, and we the pupils with lessons to learn.

"Through grace we can conquer," and the first thing we learned was: we were not alone—others had gone, or were going, through this same valley; second, when divorce comes in the Christian home, we parents need help, as well as the young people involved in the break up of a family; and third, divorce is not the "unpardonable sin." It, too, can be forgiven by our loving Heavenly Father. As with the death of a loved one, we must pass through some dark experiences before we can really minister to others in their hour of need.

For Patti the healing was long and arduous, but we all held onto Romans 8:28, believing that God in His wisdom loved us and would send good.

When God had led us through the valleys, through the darkest of nights to the "mount where the sun shines so bright," and "joy came in the morning," we recognized that God had ended our exile in those foreign lands. Now that we live on the other side of the morning, we are aware that God was walking there beside us, His heart aching with ours, wanting us to have hope, and knowing far more about it all than we did. He led us through the hot fire so we might be refined as gold is in the hands of the Goldsmith.

9

Sing! Make a Joyful Sound!

Sing! Make a joyful sound,
Sing! Life in Christ is found,
Wages of sin and death
He paid it all!
Sing! Make a joyful sound,
Sing! Life in Christ is found;
Now in my heart He reigns,
Sing! Sing! Sing![26]

Singing is a natural outpouring of joy. With music, we find peace, contentment, and quietness, as well as a means of expressing our joy and happiness.

Those in Christ have a song and can sing, whether it be a clear, accurate melody or a joyful "noise" unto the Lord. Some feel that songs and joyful sounds come only when paths are sunshiny and flower-bordered, but anytime we reflect on what God has done for us, we have reason for singing.

In this chapter, I want to stroll along memory's lane and share some of the really joyous and victorious times in our family symphony. In most symphonies, the fourth movement leads one to a cheerful and exultant frame of mind as it draws to either a triumphant or an irresistable close. That's what I hope to do with this chapter.

We often sing "Because He Lives," and my mind always goes back to when we were able to close the door on the of pain and hurt caused by the accident involving Tombo and his friends. This song will never be dearer to us than it was on a moonlit night as we drove up the Frio Canyon, about three years after the wreck.

In the months and years that have followed that period in our lives, Tombo was asked to sing and give his testimony in many churches and youth meetings. His song was "I Was Born to Serve the Lord." He would share his heart as he related the accident and Steve's death, and his own question, "Why was I left?" God had a purpose for his life—that He knew—and he must find the answer.

On this particular night, we were visiting the First Baptist Church in Leakey and, when he was asked to sing, Tombo chose the song "Because He Lives."

As he began the third verse,

> And then one day I'll cross the river;
> I'll fight life's final war with pain;
> But then as death gives way to vict'ry,
> I'll see the lights of glory and I'll know
>   He lives. . . .[27]

he broke down, tears slowly running down his cheeks. I continued playing the accompaniment. By the time the chorus began, he was able to continue singing, "Because He lives. . . ." As the chorus continued, his confidence manifested itself as he seemed to sing with a new assurance as though he *had* seen the lights.

When the service was over, as we drove out of town toward the ranch, he began explaining what had happened. "You know why I broke down? I thought about Steve and for the first time I realized that he really had 'vict'ry'; he's better off than we are. I guess I've been mad at God all these years, because He took Steve."

While he talked on and we drove along that moonbathed country road in the Texas hill country, we could literally feel a burden—a back-breaking load—being lifted, one we had not known existed in our boy's heart. I remember saying, "That's right, Tombo, we do know the song means because *Jesus* lives, but because he does live, so does Steve, and Granddaddy, and Uncle Zene, too. Someday we'll see them all."

God can take away a burden, in the twinkling of a "song." Isaiah 65:14*a* sings: "Behold, my servants shall sing for joy of heart."

What gives more joy than a wedding? Brides are a story unto themselves, but we must not leave out the groom's story either. All the weddings around our household were unique in their own right. Cynthia, being the oldest, led out.

Several times in her growing-up years she had come home to tell us excitedly, "I've found the man I'm going to marry," but when the day did arrive and she was serious, we kind of laughed.

Buryl Red had invited Cynthia to sing the solo part in the recording of the new musical, *Celebrate Life,* he and Ragan Courtney had written. She flew to Nashville for the recording sessions but did not meet Ragan until the premiere production at Ridgecrest. Buryl had mentioned to Ragan that he wanted to use Cynthia, and Ragan, not having met her, left the choice up to Buryl.

On the day she arrived home after her trip to Ridgecrest, she ran down the steps of the plane and exclaimed, "I've found the man I'm going to marry!" We smiled and asked, "OK, who is it this time?"

Hugging us with a determined look in her eyes, she answered, "Why, Ragan Courtney, the writer!"

"Oh, sure," we came back. We had only heard of him through the preadvertisements of the musical. We never dreamed a son-in-law of ours would be someone we didn't even know. Aren't All-American girls supposed to marry the All-American boy next door?

The old saying, "Love at first sight," still must be working, for later Ragan told a mutual friend of his that he had met the most wonderful girl who would surely make someone a great wife. He would love to marry her himself, but he was sure she wouldn't have *him.* The friend, who had already been talking with Cynthia, simply smiled and suggested that the two of them should get together. And they did.

By November they were engaged, and we still hadn't met our new son-in-law to be. In the next few weeks, we talked to him several times over the phone, but each time he planned a trip to San Antonio, this or that would cause him to cancel the trip. His mother, Sybil, had been in and out of the hospital for the past year, and when he would plan a trip, he would have to go to her bedside. She died the week after Christmas.

The first week in January he again planned a trip to San Antonio, but the weather wouldn't permit his coming. This time on the phone, I laughed and told him that if he didn't get there *before* the wedding, I would stop him going down the aisle and introduce myself.

Ragan finally made it two weeks before the wedding, but it wasn't until sometime later that we found out what a traumatic trip it had been for him. He was afraid that we wouldn't approve of him, especially Brother Tom the preacher.

One time Cynthia, Ragan, and Patti had been together, and he was trying to find out about his new prospective family. "Tell me about your mother and daddy," he asked.

Cynthia, with a sly grin, readily spoke up, "You know Patti? Well, Daddy is ten times worse than she is. (I need to explain here that Patti and her daddy were cut out of the same mold: headstrong, aggressive, great leadership ability, but with tremendous hearts of love for others.) Mother—you'll love." So with that kind of introduction, Ragan came that day with much "fear and trembling." And it was "love at first sight" for all of us. Brother Tom soon found in Ragan a soul buddy, and I, another dear son.

I told Ragan that day, "I don't want a son-in-law. I want another son." And, putting his arms around me, he tenderly whispered in my ear, "And I think you have come along when I needed you the most."

From the time they had announced their engagement in November, we had started the wedding plans. It would be a simple wedding at our church on February 4. Three hundred and fifty engraved wedding invitations were ordered and had arrived, but they were never to be used.

After the deaths of Cynthia's grandfather, my dad, and Ragan's mother only two weeks apart, they decided on an even smaller wedding—no invitations—and that they would be married after the morning worship service on January 28, 1973. We didn't even announce it to the church, but somehow the word leaked out, and the church was packed that morning.

It was hard for all of us, so soon after the loss of these so dear to us, but it was especially so for Ragan's father, Francis, who came to stand beside his son as best man. Their flowers were placed in a box under the front pew where they could pick them up when the time came.

Brother Tom preached on the "Christian Home," and Cynthia sang "Bless This House" and "How Great Thou Art."

When he gave an invitation at the end of his message, one lady came forward. Later, Ragan with tears in his eyes, exclaimed, "I shall never forget my wedding day. To think, a lady was saved at my wedding!" This made us love him even more because of his love and tender heart.

After the lady was presented to the church, Brother Tom stepped back to the pulpit and announced, "Ragan and Cynthia would like to culminate their morning worship with the saying of their wedding vows. You are all welcome to stay if you wish." (Not a soul moved.) And, turning to the deacons, he requested, "Gentlemen, would you please remove the altar table and pulpit? Then we will be ready."

Having preached in his sermon what he normally included in his remarks to the bride and groom, Brother Tom added a few words, pronounced them man and wife, and the ceremony was over. The next day, one of the deacon's wives reported her husband as commenting at the lunch table afterwards, "Now, that's the way to do it. Just get up and say 'I do.' "

One little boy sitting next to his grandmother spoke out loud, "Grandma, she looks like an angel!" Don't all brides look like angels?

Having planned a buffet lunch at the parsonage for the family and closest of friends, we had the usual bride's table covered with a pink-and-white net cloth, with a center of matching flowers, white candles, pink punch, and a lovely pink-and-white wedding cake.

As we were planning the menu, I asked the groom what he would like to eat, and he smilingly answered, "I don't care, as long as it is a peanut-butter-and-jelly sandwich." So, the photographer snapped a priceless picture of the bride and groom, with arms crossed, feeding each other a peanut-butter-and-jelly sandwich before they even cut their cake. There were forty to share in this happy occasion, and at the appointed hour the bride and groom left amid the rice and good wishes of all.

After living for a short time in Little Rock, Dallas, and New York, Ragan and Cynthia chose to make their home in Nashville. It was there in 1976 that Patti joined them, renting an apartment not too far from them. Only recently they moved to Louisville, Kentucky, where Ragan is on the faculty of Southern Baptist Theological Seminary.

By this time Patti was traveling with Cynthia fulltime as her accompanist, and it was more convenient for her to be near them. It is always a stirring experience, even to us parents, to see them perform, because of the affinity between the two; not necessarily because they are sisters, but because they have unity in thought through music and are sensitive to each other's moods and interpretations of songs.

Life has a manner of playing tricks on us—so goes the old adage—but sometimes when we read the blueprint God has for our lives and do not follow it, we willfully invite the "tricks."

God had picked out "Mr. Right" for Patti. Shortly after we moved to San Antonio in 1967, Patti baby-sat for a teacher friend of mine. She came home that night yelling, "I've found the boy I want to date!"

It was Scott Berry, my friend's nephew. Patti had already seen him at school but met him that night for the first time. It was two years later before they really became aware of each other again and started dating in their senior year of high school. After graduation, their paths parted as they attended different colleges. They dated off and on when they would come home from school until Patti married.

After her divorce, they once again saw each other occasionally. For eight years Scott not only loved her but was her friend and stood by her many times when she desperately needed someone.

After moving to Nashville in the fall of 1976, she made a trip back to San Antonio the next spring for Fiesta Week and once again ran into Scott. She returned to Nashville, thinking of Scott and how much she really cared for him, and was pleased when he called her on her birthday in July. The last of August they were able to be together again, and the romance blossomed once again.

One night, almost a year later, Scott called to speak to Brother Tom. He asked, "Are you going to be busy in August? I think I'm going to need a preacher about then."

Brother Tom replied, smiling at me as I stood by the phone with him, "What's the matter? Are you going to be baptized all over again?" (Brother Tom had baptized Scott when he was eighteen.)

"No," he laughingly answered, "I believe I'm going to marry this girl of yours."

At the same time that Patti and Scott's relationship was deepening, the

Lord was dealing especially in Patti's heart, and she had a renewal with Him as she became aware of how much He really cared for her. She realized how He had been patient with her through her years of doubt and struggle to work through her divorce and the days of her anguish. She realized that the Lord had gently guided her every step and had directed her to this day.

We were all in Nashville for Mother's Day 1978. Cynthia was supposed to sing at the evening services at their church, First Baptist, but her face was still swollen from some dental surgery that week, so she called the choir director, Mark Edwards, and suggested that Patti sing in her place while she accompanied her.

That night Patti stood to sing with her sister at the piano. She did a medley and ended by singing "He Was There All the Time" with much emotion and a glow about her face. It seemed everyone was moved as she sang, but for those of us who knew the whole story, it was a culmination of many years of loving, caring, waiting, and praying.

Patti later shared, "I know it's all wrapped up together, my love for the Lord and my love for Scott, too, but this is the most wonderful time of my life."

Patti wrote "A Song for You" for Scott. Cynthia set it to music, later recording it on one of her albums, "You're Welcome Here," and sang it at their wedding.

It so beautifully portrays those eight or more years:

> I can't believe I've done it!
> I've written a song for you!
> For so many years the love was there,
> But the poetry just came through.
>
> I've known all along you were best for me,
> But my heart was running free.
> Your love was laid before me,
> But I never wanted to see
> That beauty can be in unspoken words
> In unfinished symphonies;
> I felt that I must not love you
> If there wasn't a melody.

But at last I've finally done it!
For so many years the love was there,
But the poetry just came through,
I've written a song for you![28]

In August 1978 they were married in the courtyard of the First Baptist Church in San Antonio with Brother Tom officiating and the closest friends and family in attendance. Cynthia sang "A Song for You" with a harpsichord in the background.

We had one more San Antonio wedding before our family would be complete. It was fiesta time again in 1979. After the wedding, Patti and Scott had settled down there as he was finishing his last year at the University of Texas Dental School. She had gone to work at USAA and had made friends with one of the girls in her office, Debby Sacre Collins.

Fiesta Week is always a time for parties, parades, and fun, so Patti and Scott planned a patio party and decided to invite Debby for Scott's bachelor friend, Scott Bates. It didn't quite work out as they had planned. Cupid struck that night, but not with Scott and Debby—but with Tombo and Debby. He had gone back to San Antonio for fiesta Week.

When he returned to Conroe after his visit, he came in to say, "I've met the girl I want to marry!"

Since we had met Debby a few months before at a concert Cynthia had given at the Trinity Baptist Church in San Antonio, we could see why, for Debby is a altogether beautiful person. It wasn't long until we, too, had fallen in love with our new prospective daughter and looked forward to the time when she would be a part of our family.

We not only gained another daughter, but also our second grandson. Cynthia and Ragan had presented us with our first grandson, Will, in February 1979, about a month before Tombo and Debby met. Debby brought with her into the family a precious four-year-old, Nicholas. He stole our hearts when on his first visit he jumped out of the car and ran to us, calling, "Hello, Grandpa. Hello, Grandma."

A year after they met, they were married at the Little Church of La Villita, a quaint, historic church, where many young people in San

Antonio are married. Patti played the organ and again Brother Tom had the honor of performing the ceremony for the last of our three children.

I think one of the most tender moments in their ceremony was when Tombo and Debby kissed and then started to run down the aisle. They stopped, reached back to take little Nicholas by the hand and lead him down the aisle between them. He had gallantly played the part of the ring bearer and had stood quietly during the ceremony by his new Grandpa without stirring.

Later, when the pictures were being shown among our friends, someone said, "How sweet! I guess it was planned that way."

And we answered, "No, that was just two kids who knew they had a baby to take care of *before* they went on their honeymoon." They did go on their honeymoon alone, though, while Nicholas stayed with Debby's parents.

You know, grandparents can always sing and make a joyful sound about their grandchildren. We now have five: William Clawson Courtney and Lily Katherine Courtney; Matthew Courtney Berry; and Nicholas Scott Clawson (Tommy adopted him in 1981, one month before Andrew was born); and Andrew Lane Clawson.

The plurality of names was not necessarily planned, especially in Nicholas's case, since he was given the name Scott for a middle name before he came into the family. Matthew's middle name was given for his daddy, Scott Courtney Berry. When Will, our first grandchild, was born, they were still undecided about his middle name, and that night at the hospital Ragan asked if I thought Brother Tom would mind their naming him William Clawson Courtney. I told Ragan to just ask him and see how many buttons popped off his shirt.

Will, age five, contends he wants to be an actor, like his Daddy and Momma. His mother was about his age when she started dreaming of Hollywood and an acting career, as many little girls in America do.

We were not aware of her dream until she was given the opportunity of going to Hollywood and appear on the All-American College Show, in her junior year in college. She was not only in the a cappella choir, but a special group of seven singers, called the Heritage Singers. (This was organized during her freshman year, and she sang with them for the four years she was in college.) They had been asked to appear on the show. At that performance she was invited back to be a contestant as a soloist.

As most Christian parents would, we had many misgivings about the possibility of a Hollywood career, but knowing she was grown, and the decisions she would face would have to be entirely hers, with smiling faces we sent her forth.

The first time she appeared as a soloist Arthur Godfrey asked her what did her father, a Baptist preacher, think of her going to Hollywood. Cynthia, without any hesitation, answered, "He has some reservations."

Godfrey then wanted to know what she would have done if Tom had forbidden her to come. Cynthia smiled and answered, "Well, I guess I would have had to pray about that." Turning toward the camera, Godfrey quipped, "Now, Preacher, what about that answer?" This became a standing joke between the two of them, whenever she appeared on the show.

When she went for the semifinals show, it was the fall semester of her senior year at Howard Payne. As was the pattern, Mr. Godfrey asked once again about her family and her plans.

After the taping of the show, Lawrence Welk, one of the judges, came to stand by her side. He waited until nearly everyone was through with their congratulations before he commented to Cynthia, "I understand about your folks."

At first Cynthia did not quite know what he was talking about.

He continued, "I wish they were here so we could show them a good side to Hollywood. There are some fine people here." After talking with her a while, he invited her to the Palladium after the show to sing with his orchestra.

On Sunday she called, reporting that she had won. We yelled, "That's great! We're proud of you. When did you get back to Brownwood?"

"I'm not. I'm still in Hollywood."

"You'd better not be—you can't cut any more classes. What are you still doing in Hollywood?" we inquired.

Cynthia, with a smile in her voice, gave the news, "Lawrence Welk wants me to be on his show Tuesday night, so I have to stay for rehearsals tomorrow."

"Ohhh, I guess a cut in class is worth that. Don't you agree, Brother Tom?"

Without hesitating, Tom replied, "I think so!"

Later Mr. Welk had offered her a place on his show, but her reply was: "I'll have to pray about it."

Mr. Welk answered, "That's fine. We'll be praying for you out here."

Two weeks later, he called her at school to inquire about her decision. Cynthia thanked him for the opportunity to sing on his show but felt that since this was her senior year, the Lord would have her complete college before beginning her singing career. As always he was nice and agreed with her. Before he hung up, he assured her she would have a place on his show anytime she wanted it.

Two years later in the summer of 1971, she returned to Hollywood, where she appeared on the *Newcomers Show* for the summer. This time she planned to stay and pursue a career in TV. We talked for a long time the night before she left, discussing the difficulties she would face in maintaining her convictions and service to the Lord in Hollywood. She assured us it would be a mission field for her, and she felt this was what the Lord wanted her do. All we could say was, "We'll be praying for you."

As the summer drew to a close, she had become disillusioned about life and some of the people there. She could find no peace about staying. One afternoon she called, asking her daddy to fly out and to drive back with her.

After prayer meeting that Wednesday night, he left at 11 for Los Angeles. Cynthia met him at 2 AM, they drove to her hotel in Hollywood, packed the car, and pulled out about 4.

About 6 PM on Friday they pulled into our driveway. When some of our friends heard about the rushed trip, they commented, "Tom, you sure wanted to get her out of there in a hurry!"

This proved one of Brother Tom's favorite promises, Psalm 37:5. He loves to quote it thusly: "Commit thy way unto the Lord, trust also in him and [*let*] *him* bring it to pass" (author's italics). We had certainly committed Cynthia and the lure of Hollywood to Him.

The next Sunday Cynthia gave a concert at our church, and there was one song she sang just for her daddy, "Talk About a Chile, Who Do Love

Jesus—Here's One." As she sang, she looked at her daddy, and between them passed an understanding look assuring him that she and her Christian testimony were still intact, alive, and well. Brother Tom cried out, "A-A-Amen!" The girls today always declare they can locate their daddy in any crowd, if they can hear him call out "A-a-amen!" in his own special manner.

For several years Cynthia and Patti have spent the second weekend in September with the Columbus Avenue Baptist Church in Waco, helping them welcome back the Baylor students for the new year. We have been privileged to attend the last few years, since Brother Tom left the pastorate and is now in evangelism. One particular weekend stands out among the others.

Remodeling was being done on the church, so that Sunday evening the concert was to be held in the new Convention Center of Waco. During the concert, Cynthia explained that her whole family was there and, as she has done before, graciously testified, "Mother taught us all to play the piano; Daddy taught us to sing. Mother taught us Bach and Brahms, and Daddy taught us Brumley and gospel music. Patti and I would like for Daddy and our brother, Tommy, to come up and help us sing one of our family's favorite songs for you, "Just a Little Talk with Jesus."

Brother Tom and Tommy were taken by surprise, but they joined the girls on the stage. After singing, they were given a standing ovation. Dr. Marshall Edwards, then pastor of Columbus Avenue and now our pastor at First Baptist Church, Conroe, commented the other day, "They are still talking about that concert."

It may sound strange, but through music (singing) even at funerals, we have often been able to make a "joyful sound." Depending on one's outlook about death and funerals, there can often be a worship experience when a loved one dies.

One of the most touching scenes in the story of Abraham's offering of his beloved son, Isaac, unto the Lord is found in Genesis 22:5: "And, Abraham said unto his young men, Abide ye here with the ass; and *I and the lad will go yonder to worship"* (author's italics). In spite of a broken heart, a time of confusion but surrender, a time of unspoken questions, Abraham vowed that he would have a worship experience. Paul, like Abraham, wanted his departure to be one of worship. "For I am now ready to be offered, and the time of my departure is at hand" (2 Tim. 4:6). His death was to be a libation, a poured-out drink offering in worship unto his blessed Redeemer.

I remember two such funerals.

In September 1979 Scott's mother, Martha (the "Lady," as she was affectionately called by the family), who was also a dear friend of ours, died after being in the hospital less than six weeks. She had been diagnosed as having leukemia about a year before, but because Scott's father had been critically ill in the hospital most of that year, she had kept her condition from the family.

Finally, the doctor declared she was in the last stages and must go to the hospital immediately, which she did, never to return to her earthly home.

Brother Tom was asked to preach the message of consolation and hope and Cynthia was to sing. The family and friends were crushed: Martha was only fifty-two years old, so lovely and so much needed by her family.

As Brother Tom drew the message to a close, feeling led of the Lord, he asked Cynthia to sing a verse of "Brethren, We Have Met to Worship." She stood quietly and without accompaniment began to sing:

> Brethren, we have met to worship
> And adore the Lord our God;
> Will you pray with all your power,
> While we try to preach the Word?
> All is vain unless the Spirit
> Of the Holy One comes down;
> Brethren, pray and holy manna
> Will be showered all around.
> —George Atkins

And then, as though she were drawing us up to new heights nearer to the throne of God, she broke into:

> When I can read my title clear,
> To mansions in the skies,
> I'll bid farewell to ev'ry fear,
> And wipe my weeping eyes.
> —Isaac Watts

You could feel the strength of the Lord, like an electrifying current, flow through each heart, and manna fell that day.

Another time we felt music lift the sorrowing ones out of the depths of despair was at my stepfather Kelly Patrick's funeral. He passed away in August 1982, and the family gathered from far distances.

Again Brother Tom was asked to preach the message and Cynthia and Patti to sing. Grandpa Kelly had been the girls' grandfather for only a little over six years, but he had worked a special place into our hearts because of his great capacity for love. The Lord had richly blessed our lives for giving him to us, even for such a short time.

He loved Cynthia's singing and played her records over and over, even taping them on a small recorder so he could "carry her with him."

One song that delighted his heart was "Angel Band" as Cynthia sang it on her album.

The family asked the girls to sing this at the funeral. After hearing the song as Cynthia sings it, you might ask how that could be a funeral song. But hearts were transported from sorrow to worship as the girls stood, without any accompaniment, and quietly and slowly—almost as one voice—sang:

> My latest sun is sinking fast,
> My race is nearly run;
> My strongest trials now are past,
> My triumph is begun.
>
> Oh, come, angel band, come, and around me stand,
> Oh, bear me away on your snowy wings
> To my immortal home.[29]

One special joy of our life is when we are able to minister together with our children, and this has grown as they have become adults and found their own individual places of service. Whether it be revivals, concerts, weddings, or even funerals, there is a sense of completion to our family as we stand on the years of training and growing in our gifts.

As the children minister through their particular gifts, we have to admit there is a certain honor we feel as we realize we have had a part of their expanding gifts.

Someone once asked, "Do you ever get tired of being the parents of . . . ?" and we had to reply, "No, we feel it is a special gift to us." Our hearts are blessed and lifted as we worship with them while they offer their gifts to the Lord.

As the children have reached adulthood it has become more and more difficult to put all our schedules on the same time clock. It was easy when they were at home. We would load the car and go "sing," but can you imagine thirteen of us in our little Dodge Colt?

Though we do enjoy being together, we believe that now ours are individual and not family ministries.

Through the years each of the kids at different times have been with us in revivals and special occasions such as banquets, camps, and retreats, adding to our ministry.

One such revival was in Oak Shade Baptist Church at Cleveland, Texas. Brother Tom, Tombo, and I had been invited for a week's meeting. This was a first for us—to work together as an evangelistic team.

The revival meeting began, the congregational singing was over, the offering had been taken, and as Tombo stood to sing his solo, the telephone in the office rang. A deacon came for the pastor and they left. If any other pastor had left like that, not to return, we would have been shocked, but we all had been expecting this call. Carla, the pastor's daughter, was about to present him with triplets.

Tombo finished his song, and Brother Tom preached the morning message.

The community kept the lines buzzing all afternoon, while we waited for word. Late that afternoon, Jerry called to announce they had three babies: two boys and a girl.

Another revival which had an unusual beginning was in Hobbs, New Mexico. Patti was to join us and be the featured soloist for the week.

Flying from Denver, where she had been in a concert with Cynthia, she arrived Sunday afternoon around 2:00 PM. Scott had driven from San Antonio on Saturday afternoon to spend the weekend with us, so we met Patti at the airport. We were surprised to see her being helped from the plane by the hostess. In her arms was a very sick little Matthew. He had become ill in Denver and grew worse during the trip.

Feeling he needed more attention than we could give him, we rushed him to the hospital. The emergency admittance room was full, and we were shoved from one room to another, wait—wait—wait. After about two hours, while we gave him more of the medicine Patti had in her bag, his fever seemed to drop a little.

It was drawing near church time. What to do? We decided to leave. Perhaps someone at the church could help us find a doctor.

When we reached the church, it was apparent that Matthew was a little better. His fever seemed stable and he was asleep. Patti was to begin the revival with a miniconcert before her daddy preached.

We made a pallet for Matthew in the pastor's study, and I sat with him while he slept through the church service.

When Patti carried him to the doctor the next morning, he found it was an ear infection and gave him a new kind of medicine. After a couple of days Matt had all the energy any two-and-a-half year old would. We couldn't keep up with him.

I believe the revival's success began when we all joined hands to pray for a little boy and for strength to perform the task before us.

While the children were small, the invitations to sing came to the family as a unit. Only twice during their school years do we remember each member being sent an invitation. One such time was a revival in Corpus Christi. Jerry Lyons, then pastor of Southside Baptist Church, made a special effort to see that each of us had an invitation to be a part of the team, preaching and singing. Patti lived in Corpus Christi at that time. Cynthia had just returned from a summer in Hollywood. Her presence provided a good advertisement for the revival, as she appeared on Christian talk shows and other TV spots. Tombo and I joined them on the weekend.

The other time we each were invited separately was for an adult banquet at the First Baptist Church in Lockhart, some sixty miles from San Antonio. Cynthia, a student at Howard Payne, came home to go with us. It was quite an effort for all of us to get together that particular weekend. Patti had to cancel a meeting; Tombo had undergone dental work that afternoon; his mouth was still "dead" when we left. He worried about being able to sing, but he was a good trouper, and by the time we were to sing, he began to have some feeling in his mouth.

With joy and satisfaction we finished the musical program, feeling that once again the Lord had given us not only the song to sing, but the strength to give it away. As we left, we counted up the fond memories we would retain.

(I love homecomings, don't you? They are times when we gather with our family, whether our immediate family or the broader family [the church], to share in memories of times spent together.

This past year, our last pastorate, Hot Wells Baptist Church in San Antonio, gathered to celebrate their fiftieth anniversary.

Our family was there, minus Cynthia and Ragan because of schedules and distances. The Clawson Clan had been invited to sing, and we were placed last on the program.

If you have been to such a celebration, you will remember the daylong activities: church in the morning, a huge dinner-on-the-ground, and speaker after speaker in the afternoon.

The congregation did its best to stay alert and be polite to each speaker, but all that eating, plus a warm, humid, October afternoon, soon reduced them to an inattentive, torpid state.

It was about 4 when Brother Tom, Tombo, Nicholas, and I stood to sing. Suddenly, Patti at the piano, with a fast tempo and an accented beat, began a syncopated introduction to the old gospel song, "I'm Standing on the Solid Rock." Never have we seen a quicker response than that congregation, coming alive, gave us—vocal, spiritual, and a little physical!)

Brother Tom sang at that banquet in Lockhart "He Touched Me," which had a special meaning for him about that time.

Within the very month of the banquet, Brother Tom had located an old Marine buddy he had not seen or heard of in almost twenty-five years.

Nothing unusual—oh, but there was. You see, for the three years-plus Tom had been in the Marine Corps and overseas, he had "walked away from the Lord; dishonoring his name; living the life that no Christian should; giving a negative witness or no witness at all," as he recalled. In the summer of 1946 he had made a new committal to Jesus as Lord of his life and from that day has tried to live as close to him as possible.

If the song "He Touched Me" had been written then, Brother Tom's song for the last thirty-eight years would have been:

> Since I met this blessed Savior,
> Since He cleansed and made me whole,
> I will never cease to praise Him,
> I'll shout it while eternity rolls.[30]

Locating his friend was one of those unusual times when you throw a name into the conversation, and you find how small the world really is.

Brother Tom was talking to his secretary, and several other ladies in the office when one of them, Mary Couch, mentioned that she was from Hammond, Louisiana. Tom told her he had had a buddy in the Marine Corps from Ponchatoula. She remarked that the two towns were right next to each other.

After making a trip home a short time after that conversation, Mary came back and told Brother Tom, "I located Gerald for you."

"Oh," he replied, looking at her rather surprised, as if he weren't sure what she was talking about. "Who?"

"You know, Gerald Methvin."

"Oh, sure," he smiled interested in her report. "I'm sorry. I didn't know who you were talking about at first. We always called him Methvin."

In a few days, a letter arrived from Louisiana and it said, "Boy, was I surprised to hear that you are a Reverend!"

Brother Tom treasures this letter, especially the closing line where Methvin wrote, "Old Buddy, pray for me." And we have.

A month later we visited in his home on our way to the Southern Baptist Convention in New Orleans (1969). As we sat in their kitchen, preparing shrimp salad and frying fresh catfish Cajun style, Brother Tom told Methvin what had really occurred in 1946, when Jesus touched his life and forgave him for almost four wasted years.

Other Marine Corps friends' paths have crossed Brother Tom's. He has tried to share with each one who changed his life. One experience he particularly likes telling about happened at San Antonio's Baptist Memorial Hospital in December of 1968.

It was the day for hospital visits. Rather than parking in the lot out front, Brother Tom decided to slip into a space near the side entrance. It would be closer to the room where he planned to visit.

He first saw the man walking across the doctors' parking lot. *Where have I seen him before?* pondered Brother Tom. *I know I know him from somewhere. Oh, well, it'll come to me after a while.*

Looking at his watch, Brother Tom saw it was almost lunchtime. He decided he might as well eat before he left the hospital. After eating, he rose and headed for the racks to put away his empty tray. Then he saw that man again, coming in the door. He thought, *Two times . . . that's just too much.* Putting the tray in the slot, he turned and walked toward the man. He stuck out his hand and introduced himself, "I'm Tom Clawson. Don't I know you?"

The man looked at him without smiling, ignoring the outstretched hand. He said, "Your face isn't familiar to me, and your name doesn't mean anything to me, either." Right friendly like!

"Well, I've seen you somewhere. I saw you coming across the doctor's parking lot. Are you a doctor?

"Oh, noooo . . ." he answered, as if to say "not *me.*"

Brother Tom, still trying to conjure up a name, continued, "I'm the pastor of the Hot Wells Baptist Church and thought maybe we had met at some meeting. Are you a preacher?"

"Hardly," he returned, "but I am a Baptist. I go to the Southeast Baptist Church."

"No," Brother Tom said, "I've not been out there that I remember."

They ran through the names of several towns, churches, schools—no connections. Finally, Brother Tom, figuring they were about the same age, questioned him about his military service during the Second World War. "What branch of service were you in?"

"The Marines—Third Division," the man answered.

"Say, your bunch was set up down from us on the Canal at Tassfaranga. I was in the 1st MAC Motor."

And, with a startled look on his face, the man pointed his finger at Brother Tom, exclaiming, "I know you! I used to buy my hooch from you!"

"Yeah, that's me—I was the company bootlegger!" laughed Brother Tom. "That's where I saw you—on Guadalcanal. Can you believe that—twenty-five years ago!"

They laughed and then the man gave his name—Milton Johnson—and said, "So, you're a preacher now? Times do change, don't they?"

"People do," came back Brother Tom. "When the Lord gets hold of you, He can change even an old bootlegger into a preacher. Say, you ought to come out and let me preach at you sometime."

"I just might do that one of these days," replied Milton. They talked some more and then parted. Roads cross in the strangest places.

The next afternoon, having studied all morning and needing a little diversion, Brother Tom went out to work in his roses. He was down on his knees, digging around the roots and repacking the earth at the base of the roses, when he looked up to see one of our church members drive up to the fence and jump out all excited-like. She ran up to the fence and exclaimed, "Brother Tom, what's this I hear about you being a bootlegger?"

He smiled rather foolishly and asked, "Sharon, where did you hear that?"

"Well," she answered, "Frank (her husband) was at work last night, and this young man who has come to work at the funeral home told him, 'My uncle had a funny experience this morning. He met a preacher who used to be his bootlegger!

"Frank asked him what the preacher's name was and the kid said, 'I don't know, but he pastors this Hot Wells Baptist Church over here,' pointing toward the east.

"And Frank said,'Hey, that's my church and that must be my pastor!'"

"Brother Tom," smiled Sharon, "Were you really a bootlegger?"

Brother Tom laughed and held up his hands, "Yeah, Sharon, I guess you've got me! But that was a *long* time ago, and I have changed, don't you think?"

They had a good laugh, talked about what a change the Lord brings into people's lives, and Sharon said, "Well, I guess I had better be

going—I got to fix supper for Frank before he goes back to work tonight.
Be seeing you, Brother Tom. Make those roses grow pretty," she remarked as she drove off.

Brother Tom kept working in the roses and reminiscing about those
years so long ago, and that life which seemed far away and yet so near,
and he thought of the first verse of the song, "He Touched Me."

> Then the hand of Jesus touched me
> And now I am no longer the same.

But the story does not end there.

Some time passed before Milton and Mrs. Johnson visited Hot Wells
to hear Brother Tom preach. The Sunday morning they visited Brother
Tom introduced him and said, "Remember I told you about meeting one
of my old bootlegger customers? Well, this is the man." I think Mrs.
Johnson wanted to crawl under the bench, but we all had a good laugh.

A couple of years later, Tombo was music and youth director at First
Baptist Church in Nixon, seventy miles south of San Antonio. When the
visitors were introduced one Sunday morning, he recognized Milton
Johnson and after the service, went back to welcome him to Nixon.
Milton was waiting for him and inquired, "Do you remember me?"

Tombo assuringly answered, "Yes, you were my Daddy's 'customer'!"
He remembered him from Milton's visit at Hot Wells.

They visited a few minutes on the front steps of the church, and the
Johnsons mentioned that they had some property in the Nixon vicinity.

It is strange that every couple of years or so, our paths have crossed
only for a few minutes each time. Each time we are once again made
aware of the graciousness of the Lord in the changes that can come into
a person's life.

The next time we heard of Milton was at a revival in a suburb of San
Antonio. One night Brother Tom told this story to illustrate how our
past often catches up with us and how "Jesus touches" us, to give us a
new present and future in him.

After the service, one of the men of the church asked Brother Tom,
"Did you know that Milton Johnson is one of my best friends, and have
you heard what they did to him?"

"No, what? And who are 'they'?" asked Brother Tom, smiling at him.
"He moved to Nixon and joined the church there, and now they made
a deacon out of him!"

"Well, praise the Lord. Tell him 'hi,' will you?" requested Brother
Tom.

The next year, we were at the evangelism conference in Fort Worth
when Brother Tom saw Milton walking down the hall as if he were
looking for someone. Tom wasn't able to get to him for the crowd, and
Milton walked on down the hall. In a few minutes, Milton was back, and
this time Brother Tom managed to step out in front of him and laughingly ask, "What's a bootlegger's customer doing at a place like this?"

Milton smiled and replied, "The same thing that an old bootlegger is
doing here—trying to soak up some of this good preaching!" They
embraced and both yelled about the same time, "Praise the Lord!"

Then he asked, "Did you hear what 'they' did to me?"

Brother Tom said, "Yeah, but I want to hear it from you."

They talked awhile, as they shared some of the things that had been
happening in their lives.

Some time later, we heard Milton was serving on the pulpit committee
in his church.

Their relationship has been only in short, fleeting moments, such as
their first meeting many years ago, but now there is a bond that can only
be found in Christ. In our Christian pilgrimage our paths cross and
recross with other pilgrims who add a new dimension to our lives and
we to theirs. God steers them our way so we might "bump" into them,
for He knows we each have something to share with others, to enrich
our lives, to make us aware of a tremendous truth, or perhaps to show
us how small we are in God's overall plan for His children.

It is easy to "sing and make a joyful sound" when we recall the
manifold blessings which have been ours, as each of us have used the
song God gave. Together we tried faithfully to put our gifts into service
not only to enrich our lives, and to bring pleasure and encouragement
to others, but to give back our multiplied gifts to the Lord!

Epilogue
The Last Movement . . .

. . . has not been played; "the song still goes on."

Our family life has indeed been a "symphony," having many characteristics of a real symphonic poem, as we have experienced all the emotions stirred by the music. Like the fourth movement of a symphony, our life has increased in momentum and complexities, since we are no longer one family, but with the extended families, we are now four. David said, "As arrows are in the hand of a mighty man; so are the children of the youth. Happy is the man that hath his quiver full of them" (Ps. 127:4-5). Our "other three children" have been added, and now the five grandchildren have come along giving joy to our "old age."

Like sturdy, healthy branches, the three children (now adults with their families) go out from the stem—"Mama and Papa." We are still a family—a family symphony—as we each continue to sing the song given us many years ago. And we pray that it will go on and on.

> So I'll sing and never tire, and I'll run and not grow weary,
> 'Cause even in my human weakness, as long as God gives me breath,
> I will walk and never wander.
> And I'll laugh when the world calls me fool.
> 'Cause I know, I know where I am going.
> I know in Jesus I belong,
> So, as long as God gives breath I'll sing His song.[31]

Notes

1. From "Life Is a Symphony" by Beatrice Bush Bixler © Copyright 1944. Renewal 1971 by Beatrice Bush Bixler. Assigned to Singspiration, Division of the Zondervan Corporation. All rights reserved. Used by permission.

2. Black spiritual—author unknown, public domain

3. By Robert Harkness—now public domain

4. From "God Gave the Song" (from "Alleluia") by William J. Gaither, Gloria Gaither, Ronn Huff. © Copyright 1973 by William J. Gaither and Paragon Music Corp. Used by permission.

5. From "The Journey" by Ragan Courtney and Cynthia Clawson © Copyright 1977 Triune Music, Inc. Used by permission.

6. From "The Truth Will Make You Free" by Ragan Courtney © Copyright 1972 Broadman Press. All rights reserved. International copyright secured.

7. From "That's What It's All About"—unable to locate writer and company

8. From "His Way, Mine" by Dick and Bo Baker. Copyright © 1971 Crescendo Music Publications, Inc. Reprinted by permission of publisher.

9. From "I Like Bananas" by Kamalei Mark Tewes. Used by special permission of the composer.

10. From "His Music" by George Gagliardi. © Copyright 1977 Triune Music, Inc. Used by special permission.

11. From "The Family of God" by William J. and Gloria Gaither. © Copyright 1970 by William J. Gaither. Used by permission.

12. Words by Stuart K. Hine © Copyright 1953, 1955, Renewed 1981 by Manna Music, Inc.

13. From "Stop This Haulin' Water to the Sea" by Reba Rambo and Dony McGuire © Copyright 1980 by Lexicon Music/Makanume Music ASCAP All rights reserved. International copyright secured. Used by special permission.

14. From "Let Others See Jesus in You" by B. B. McKinney © Copyright

1924. Renewal 1952 Broadman Press. All rights reserved. International copyright secured.

15. From "I Don't Have to Wait" by Harold Deal and Harry Dixon Loes—now public domain

16. Words by James Rowe

17. © 1953 Irving Berlin. Renewed 1981.

18. From "He Saw Me" by Debbie Johnston. © Copyright 1974. Used by special permission.

19. From "God Leads His Dear Children Along" by G. A. Young—now public domain

20. From "Joy Comes in the Morning" by William J. and Gloria Gaither. © Copyright 1974 by William J. Gaither. Used by permission.

21. From the poem "My Lamp Is Shattered"—source unknown

22. From "God Gave the Song" (from "Alleluia") by William J. Gaither, Gloria Gaither, Ron Huff. © Copyright 1973 by William J. Gaither and Paragon Music Corp. Used by permission.

23. From "It Is Well With My Soul" by H. G. Spafford and P. P. Bliss—now public domain

24. From "He Sends the Rainbow with the Rain" by B. B. McKinney. © Copyright 1931. Renewal 1959 Broadman Press. All rights reserved. International copyright secured.

25. From "Thank You, Lord" by Dan Burgess © Copyright 1972 by Lexicon Music, Inc. ASCAP All rights reserved. International copyright secured. Used by Special Permission.

26. From "Sing! Make a Joyful Sound" by Joe Liles. © Copyright 1962 by Singspiration, Inc. All rights reserved. Used by permission.

27. From "Because He Lives" by William J. and Gloria Gaither. © Copyright 1971 by William J. Gaither. Used by permission.

28. From "A Song for You" by Patti Clawson Berry and Cynthia Clawson. © Copyright 1983. Triune Music, Inc. Used by Special Permission.

29. From "Angel Band" by J. Hascall and William B. Bradbury. Arranged by Marshall Morgan. © Copyright 1983 Triune Music, Inc. Used by Special Permission.

30. From "He Touched Me" by William J. Gaither. © Copyright 1963 by William J. Gaither. Used by permission.

31. From "So I'll Sing" by Lilly Green © Copyright 1977 and arr. © 1979 by Word Music, Inc. All rights reserved. International Copyright Secured. Used by Permission.

Serving in God's Symphony

Here is a chronological listing of the places where we have lived and the churches where we have served. As we ramble through the years in our story, maybe this will help you with the time frames.

1946-1953—Houston, Texas

(with six months in the Marine Corps during the Korean War, October 1950—April 1951, Camp Pendleton and Fallbrook, California)

1953-1955—Corpus Christi, Texas

Students, University of Corpus Christi

Aransas Pass, Texas, Greewood Baptist Church—music director and pianist

Pastor, Brewster Street Chapel, later called Central Baptist Mission of the Downtown Baptist Church, Corpus Christi, Texas

1955-1956—Walnut Creek, California

First Southern Baptist Church, music director, pianist, men's Bible class (while student at Golden Gate Seminary)

1956-1957—Pacific Grove, California

Pastor, Del Monte Park Baptist Church

1957-1958—Houston, Texas

Associate Pastor and minister of education, Broadway Baptist Temple

1958-1959—Yoakum, Texas

Pastor, Progress Baptist Church

1959-1960—Pleasanton, Texas

Associate Pastor and minister of education, First Baptist Church

1960-1963—Jewett, Texas

Pastor, First Baptist Church

1963-1967—Houston, Texas
Pastor, Southeast Baptist Church
1967-1976—San Antonio, Texas
Pastor, Hot Wells Baptist Church
1976—Conroe, Texas
Vocational evangelist